TIME WILL ONLY TELL

by Lawrence Veltkamp

The contents of this work, including, but not limited to, the accuracy of events, people, and places depicted; opinions expressed; permission to use previously published materials included; and any advice given or actions advocated are solely the responsibility of the author, who assumes all liability for said work and indemnifies the publisher against any claims stemming from publication of the work.

Cover art by Victor Solis III

Dorrance Publishing Co
585 Alpha Drive
Pittsburgh, PA 15238
Visit our website at www.dorrancebookstore.com

ISBN: 978-1-6393-7258-4
eISBN: 978-1-6393-7658-2

CHAPTER 1

The days in history become the time of each event. The dates in history are the days that become the creation of a nation. Is it possible for the two dates to parallel in time? When an event happens on a specific date, it becomes destiny. That's what history is, the future!

History in America, the Revolutionary War, the Declaration of Independence, the Constitution, the War of 1812, the Mexican-American war, slavery, the Civil War, Segregation, World War I, World War II, the Korean War, the Vietnam War, the Civil Rights Act of 1964, the Voting Rights Act of 1965 (August 6) and the Persian Gulf War.

History in America, George Washington, John Adams, Thomas Jefferson, James Madison, and James Monroe, the founding fathers of America, the 56 signers of the Declaration of Independence, the 39 signers of the Constitution, and four presidents assassinated throughout history.

On June 28, 1776, a committee of five drafted the Declaration of Independence in Philadelphia. Written by Thomas Jefferson, who became the future third president of the United States, and then edited by the coauthors John Adams, who became the second president of the United States, Benjamin Franklin, Roger Sherman, and Robert Livingston.

On July 2, 1776, Congress voted to declare independence from Great Britain. Two days later, on July 4, the Continental Congress declared independence, approving a final draft and adopting the Declaration of Independence.

When Thomas Jefferson wrote the Declaration of Independence, he wrote, "All men are created equal, that they are endowed by their Creator with certain unalienable rights, that among these are life, liberty and the pursuit of happiness."

In Philadelphia, at the Gettysburg address, Abraham Lincoln spoke on November 19, 1863, "Fourscore and seven years our fathers brought forth on this continent, a new nation, conceived in liberty, and dedicated to the proposition that all men are created equal."

Joseph Bradley Varnum, a United States Senator from Massachusetts, on March 3, 1805, proposed to amend the Constitution and abolish the slave trade. Two years after Joseph Brady Varnum presented the Slave Trade Act, Thomas Jefferson signed the Transatlantic Slave trade Act on March 3, 1807, which became law on January 1, 1808. It prohibited new enslaved people from being imported into the United States.

Precisely 30 years after Thomas Jefferson signed the Transatlantic Slave Trade Act, Abraham Lincoln made one of his first protests against slavery on March 3, 1837.

In the Illinois Gen. Assembly, Abraham Lincoln made one of his first public declarations against slavery. The protest went to the House floor when it was read and then sent off for publication.

"They believe that the institution of slavery is founded on both injustice and bad policy; but that the promulgation of abolition doctorates tends rather to increase than to abate its evils. They believe that the Congress of the United States has no power, under the Constitution, to interfere with the institution of slavery and the different states. They believe that the Congress of the United States has the power, under the Constitution, to abolish slavery in the District of Columbia, but that power will not be exercised unless and to the request of the people of said district. The difference between these options and those contained in the said resolutions is there is a reason for entering this protest." - Abraham Lincoln, Representative of the County of Sangamon.

"The Star-Spangled Banner" was chosen as the official tune to be played at the raising of the flag by the Secretary of the Navy, Benjamin F. Tracy, on July 26, 1889. Robert Lincoln, Abraham Lincoln's only son to live past eighteen years, died July 26, 1926. 1916, President Woodrow Wilson signed an executive order for the Star-Spangled Banner to be played at military and other suitable events. Abraham Lincoln was the sixteenth President of the United States, and Abraham Lincoln died on April 15, 1865. On April 15, 1929, Rep. John Linthicum proposed legislation that made the Star-Spangled Banner the National Anthem. On March 3, 1837, Abraham Lincoln made one of his first protests against slavery. On March 3, 1931, The Star-Spangled Banner became the American National Anthem, signed by the thirty-first President Herbert Hoover.

55 years after the Transatlantic Slave Trade Act was in effect on January 1, 1808, The 16th President, Abraham Lincoln, issued the emancipation proclamation on January l, 1863. The first president George Washington and the fourth president James Madison were the two future U.S. presidents that presented the Constitution to the United States. George Washington stood as the President of the Constitutional Congress on September 17, 1787, when 39 delegates signed the Constitution.

The Father of the Constitution, James Madison, wrote the document that formed the Constitution. On June 8, 1789, James Madison `presented and proposed the Bill of Rights to Congress precisely 56 years before Andrew Jackson passed away on June 8, 1845. There stood 56 signers of the Declaration of Independence.

In the Revolutionary War, Jackson joined a militia when he was 13 years old and then captured by the British beside his brother Robert in 1781, when Jackson refused to shine a British Soldier's boots. They slashed his face and hand, which left a permanent scar. There were 13 original Colonies.

The third president, Thomas Jefferson, and the second president, John Adams became the Author and co-author of the Declaration of Independence. The future fifth president, James Monroe, became wounded in the Battle of Trenton on December 26, 1776, after crossing The Delaware River with George Washington. James Monroe died on July 4, 1831, exactly five years after Thomas Jefferson and John Adams, who died on July 4, 1826.

CHAPTER 2

THE DUEL – ALEXANDER HAMILTON AND ARRON BURR

The lead-up to the famous Hamilton-Burr duel.

Alexander Hamilton and Arron Burr became rivals in 1791. Burr was elected by the legislature as a Senator from New York, defeating the Incumbent General Philip Schuyler, Alexander Hamilton's father-in-law.

In the presidential election of 1800, with 73 electoral votes each, Thomas Jefferson and Aaron Burr were in a virtual tie for President and Vice President.

Alexander Hamilton, still angry about the 1791 election, preferred Thomas Jefferson as President over Burr, so he convinced more than a few Federalists to change their support to Jefferson, allowing Jefferson to win the presidency on the 36-ballot, meaning Aaron Burr became Thomas Jefferson's vice president.

Then In the 1804 presidential election, the 12th Amendment changed the process whereby a president and the vice president become elected. The new election process made the President and vice-President run on one ticket, and The United States first used the twelfth Amendment in the 1804 election.

After the Twelfth Amendment became law, Thomas Jefferson wanted a different running mate other than Aaron Burr. Burr recognized he would not remain Thomas Jefferson's vice president, so he switched political parties in early 1804 and attempted to become the Governor of New York. He intended to run as a Federalist, which was Hamilton's party that contested the very thought of Burr's Federalist ambition. To keep it simple, Burr decided to run as an Independent instead.

In February 1804, Hamilton gave a speech regarding the New York governor's election, calling Burr unfit, dangerous, and despicable. Charles P. Cooper wrote a letter to Alexander Hamilton's father-in-law Philip Schuyler about the speech.

The New York governor's election occurred in April, and Aaron Burr lost.

After the New York governor's election, the letter to Philip Schuyler got published in Albany, New York. Aaron Burr demanded an apology for the slander said about him. Hamilton refused. They exchanged letters, eventually leading to the famous duel on July 11, 1804, in Weehawken, New Jersey, where Alexander Hamilton became wounded and died the next day, July 12, 1804.

Do the dates parallel in history?

Every 20 years for 140 years, each President who became elected when the year ended with a zero would die before his term was over:

Zachary Taylor, the twelfth president, was elected in 1848 and died while he was in office in 1850.

CHAPTER 3

The ninth president, William Henry Harrison, elected in 1840, died in Washington, DC, on April 4, 1841.

The sixteenth president Abraham Lincoln elected in 1860, died on April 15, 1865, in Washington DC — assassinated.

The twentieth president James Garfield elected in 1880, died September 19, 1881, in Washington DC — assassinated.

The twenty-fifth president William McKinley elected in 1900, died September 14, 1901, in Buffalo, New York — assassinated.

The twenty-ninth president Warren G. Harding, elected in 1920, died August 2, 1923, in San Francisco, California — his death was unclear, either a heart attack or a stroke.

The thirty-second president Franklin Delano Roosevelt, elected in 1940, died on April 12,

1945 in Warm Springs, Georgia. Franklin Roosevelt died of a cerebral hemorrhage.

The thirty-fifth president John F Kennedy elected in 1960, died on November 22, 1963, in Dallas, Texas — assassinated.

The third president, Thomas Jefferson, who won the 1800 election, died July 4, 1826; The fifth president, James Monroe, who won reelection in 1820, died July 4, 1831. Thomas Jefferson and James Monroe did not die while they were in office, yet they passed on July 4, precisely five years from one another. The zero years in which they became elected are perfect parallels that match each President selected on a zero year and then intersected one hundred years from one another. Starting with William Henry Harrison in 1840, if the President became elected on a zero year, that President would die before leaving office.

John Adams and Thomas Jefferson died on the same day, July 4, 1826, Exactly Fifty years after the Declaration of Independence.

James Monroe died July 4, 1831, 5 years after John Adams and Thomas Jefferson.

Thomas Jefferson in the 1800 election. elected

William McKinley in the 1900 election. Re-elected

James Monroe in 1820. Re-elected

Warren G Harding in 1920. elected

William Henry Harrison in 1840. elected

Franklin Roosevelt in 1940. Re-elected

Abraham Lincoln in 1860. elected

John F. Kennedy in 1960. elected

James Garfield in 1880. elected

Ronald Regan in 1980. Elected

CHAPTER 4

William McKinley died on September 14, 1901.

Thomas Jefferson died on July 4, 1826.

Thomas Jefferson in 1800 elected.

William McKinley, in 1900 re-elected.

Thomas Jefferson fell into a depression on September 6, 1782, when his wife Martha died 19 years before he became the third president. On September 6, 1901, William McKinley was shot and wounded by an anarchist 119 years after Martha Jefferson died. Thomas Jefferson's first vice president Aaron Burr died September 14, 1836. William McKinley died September 14, 1901. September 14, 1901, Theodore Roosevelt became the 26th president of the United States.

The twenty-fifth president William McKinley, wounded on September 6, 1901, was in Buffalo, New York gathering with a long line of spectators when Leon Czolgosz, a 28-year-old man from Detroit, shot McKinley twice. One bullet hit the twenty-fifth president's button that, blocked the bullet. The other bullet hit his stomach and went into his pancreas. When McKinley fell back into a security guard, he said, "My wife be careful how you tell her — oh, be careful," he said. After eight days in the hospital and two operations, McKinley died on September 14, 1901. Thomas Jefferson was born on April 13, 1743.

James Benjamin Parker's death certificate reads April 13, 1907. James Benjamin Parker was a six-foot-six inch and approximately 250-pound African American man from Savannah, Georgia, who Knocked Leon Czolgosz's gun to the ground, which prevented him from shooting McKinley a third time. McKinley was the last Civil War Veteran among the presidents who fought in the Civil War. He served in the 23rd Ohio Volunteers under the future nineteenth president, Rutherford B Hayes. McKinley followed the sixteenth president's leadership. McKinley's beliefs were to preserve the Union and end Involuntary Servitude, just like Lincoln's beliefs.

Thomas Jefferson owned more than 600 enslaved people throughout his lifetime, more than any other president. Thomas Jefferson married Martha Wayles Jefferson, the half-sister of Sally Hemmings. Sally Hemmings was half African-American.

Thomas Jefferson inherited Many enslaved people through the family. He seldom bought enslaved people, even though he owned more than 600 enslaved people throughout his life when he wrote the Declaration of Independence in 1776. He wrote a passage that the Second Continental Congress deleted, which was a paragraph that was antislavery —

> "He waged cruel war against human nature itself, violating its most sacred rights of life and liberty in the persons of a distant people who never offended him, captivating & carrying them into slavery in another hemisphere or to incur miserable death in their transportation thither. This piratical warfare, the opprobrium of infidel powers, is the warfare of the Christian king of Great Britain. Determined to keep open a market where men should be prohibited or restrain this execrable commerce. And that this assemblage of horrors might want no fact distinguished die, he is now exciting those very people to rise in arms among us and to purchase that liberty of which he has deprived them by murdering the people on whom he has to obtrude them: thus paying off

> former crimes committed against the Liberties of one people, with crimes which he urges them to commit against the lives of another."—Thomas Jefferson

1800-1900 election of Thomas Jefferson to William McKinley.

The third president, Thomas Jefferson's wife, Martha Jefferson, died on September 6.

The twenty-fifth president William McKinley on September 6, 1901, was shot.

CHAPTER 5

Gilbert Lafayette was born on September 6, 1757. Frances Wright was born on September 6, 1795. 38 years apart.

Gilbert Lafayette was born, in Chavaniac, France, on September 6, 1757. Lafayette fought in the Revolutionary War for America's Independence, becoming a Major General for the U.S. He was also a Lieutenant General for France. In America, Lafayette fought and then became wounded in Pennsylvania at the Battle of Brandywine. The other battles that Lafayette fought included The Battle of Gloucester, the action of Valley Forge, the Battle of Barton Hill, the Battle of Rhode Island, the Battle of Monmouth, and the Battle of, the Movement of Yorktown, where he fought for American independence. On September 17, 1781, Washington granted Lafayette control of the American forces at Yorktown. Gen. Barton von Steuben and John Peter Gabriel Muhlenberg, under Lafayette's authority and about 5000 men, blocked Cornwallis's exit by land out of Yorktown. The French Navy had already rejected Cornwallis's awaited reinforcements at sea when the Battle of Virginia Capes ensued on September 5. Cornwallis's navy was overwhelmed, and Cornwallis became trapped at Yorktown. George Washington, with 2,500 troops, and the French forces commanded by Rochambeau, with about 4000 soldiers, made a 200-mile journey from New York to Virginia and met up with Lafayette on September 14 to complete any thought of Cornwallis escaping. On September 28, The French Navy added more troops.

On October 19, 1781, Cornwallis officially surrendered.

Gilbert Lafayette believed in independence, so he fought for the cause of freedom for all people without discrimination. Lafayette as an abolitionist, came up with an idea to liberate the enslaved people.

George Washington received a note concerning Lafayette's idea; Lafayette sought-after Washington's support. Washington's slaves would be free tenants on land they would work on, and the two would buy. Lafayette hoped his project would succeed in the United States and spread into the West Indies.

Lafayette expressed the passionate statement that "If it is a wild scheme, I would rather be mad in this way than die wise and the other task." Washington responded warmly but preferred to discuss the details in person; he explained the scheme. "Which you propose as a precedent to encourage the patience of the black people of this country from that state of bondage and which they are held, and are striking evidence of the benevolence of your heart. I shall be happy to join you in such laudable work but will differ going into the details of the business till I have the pleasure of seeing you."

Washington turned down Lafayette's invitation to join him, but he commended Lafayette for his character and support of the enslaved.

On July 11, 1789, Lafayette drafted the Declaration of the Rights of Man and the Citizen for France with Thomas Jefferson's assistance.

In 1783, Lafayette envisioned an entitlement to an estate in South America in the French colony of Cayenne that he eventually purchased. He intended to liberate enslaved workers through gradual liberation. He wanted his example to help end slavery. Lafayette's friend Francis Wright was born September 6, 1795, in Scotland. Francis Wright was also an abolitionist who created the Nashoba population in Tennessee. The Nashoba community was to educate and prepare enslaved people for emancipation.

CHAPTER 6

When Lafayette accompanied Francis Wright and her sister Camilla around America in 1824, Wright expressed to Lafayette that she wanted to obtain enslaved people, so she could set up a free society to establish a self-sufficient environment where enslaved people could live free—an idea motivated by Lafayette, given that he formed his community himself. Previous presidents Jefferson and Madison, along with James Monroe, became enlightened of Francis's intentions when Wright and Lafayette stopped at their residences. Francis then started her journey and arrived in Memphis, Tennessee, in early October 1825. She researched the land along the Wolf River, where she purchased 1940 acres of land with 11 enslaved people to reside in a self-maintained community. Francis labored hard with her slaves to create the community, but then she had to quit working and step away because she became seriously Ill with malaria. Her sister Camilla took charge when Francis became sick.

Camilla married in 1827 and gave James Richardson, a helper, control of Nashoba's operations. Francis was unable to stay at Nashoba due to her health problems.

One hundred and twenty years after Francis Wright was born on September 6, 1795, William Henry West died on September 6, 1915. William Henry West, an African-American police officer in Washington D.C., became the only police officer in history to arrest a sitting president, Ulysses S Grant, for exceeding his horse and buggy to an unacceptable high speed. Grant received a speeding ticket the day before from West.

CHAPTER 7

George Eacker was friends with Aaron Burr Junior before he shot Philip Hamilton. George Eacker died January 4, 1804, on Aaron Burr's senior's birthday, January 4, 1716. Aaron Burr Senior was the father of Aaron Burr Junior, who shot Alexander Hamilton. Alexander Hamilton was the father of Philip Hamilton.

Aaron Burr Senior was born on January 4, 1716. He was one of the co-founders of the College of New Jersey, today known as Princeton University. He was an honorable Presbyterian Minister and a college instructor who was the father of Aaron Burr, the third vice president of the United States under Thomas Jefferson.

Aaron Burr Senior died September 24, 1757, when his son was only two. Aaron Burr Junior was still with his mother, Esther Edwards, who passed away the following year on April 7, 1758. She died less than a month after her father's death. Her father was supposed to come to Princeton to be Burr's replacement as the college president. George Eacker, who killed Philip Hamilton, died of tuberculosis on January 4, 1804.

George Eacker graduated from Columbia in New York City, where he studied law as an apprentice to Henry Livingston. Eacker became a famous New York attorney associated with the democratic—Republican party.

He became good friends with Aaron Burr, who assembled Tammany Hall, the first effective political machine in the U.S. Eacker's connection with Burr left Eacker and Alexander Hamilton distrusting one another.

George Eacker made a political Fourth of July speech regarding Alexander Hamilton. George Eacker's speech was also at odds with Alexander Hamilton's son, Philip. After Eacker's speech, Four Months later, Philip and his friend Stephen Price found Eacker while he was watching a play. The two men criticized Eacker. Eacker called the two men "damn radicals," they insulted one another, resulting in a challenge to a duel.

First, the 27-year-old Eacker faced Stephen Price on November 22, 1801, in Weehawken, New Jersey. Four shots exchanged fired, but neither party was injured. The next day, in Weehawken, NJ, Philip met his destiny when the bullet of George Eacker went through his body into his left arm; he died the next day. Phillip died in the exact location where his father, Alexander, would die in a duel with Aaron Burr in 1804. George Eacker was a volunteer firefighter—two months following George Eacker's duel with Phillip Hamilton. George was acting with his volunteer fire unit putting out a fire when he caught a cold that advanced into tuberculosis. He would struggle with the ailment for the next two years. Finally, in 1804, Eacker passed away at 30 years old.

Thomas Jefferson and William McKinley were elected when the year ended with 00.

Thomas Jefferson's wife, Martha Jefferson, died on September 6, 1782.

William McKinley, on September 6, 1901, was shot.

Marquis Lafayette, the war hero of two nations and an abolitionist, was born on September 6, 1757.

Frances Wright, an abolitionist, was born on September 6, 1795.

CHAPTER 8

William McKinley died September 14, 1901. Thomas Jefferson's first VP, Aaron Burr Junior, died September 14, 1836. William McKinley V.P. Theodore Roosevelt became the 26th President on September 14, 1901.

In the Aaron Burr duel with Alexander Hamilton, Alexander Hamilton died on July 12, 1804.

Theodore Roosevelt Junior, the son of the twenty-sixth president, died July 12, 1944

The son of Alexander Hamilton, Philip Hamilton, who dueled with George Eacker, died November 24, 1801. William McKinley Senior, the father of the twenty-fifth president, died November 24, 1892.

George Eacker died on January 4, 1804, on Aaron Burr Senior's birthday, January 4, 1716. Aaron Burr Senior was the father of Aaron Burr Junior.

The twenty-sixth president, Theodore Roosevelt, died on January 6, 1919.

Thomas Lincoln, the father of the sixteenth president, was born on January 6, 1778.

Theodore Roosevelt Senior died February 9, 1878, and was born September 22, 1831. The Preliminary Emancipation was September 22, 1862.

On February 9, 1861, Jefferson Davis was elected provisional President of the Confederacy. William Henry Harrison, the ninth president who only served 32 days and then died while he was in office, was born February 9, 1773, and died April 4, 1841. John Burr, who was half African-American and the son of Aaron Burr, passed away on April 4, 1864.

Martin Luther King died on April 4, 1968.

fate

Stephen Douglas of Illinois introduced the Kansas-Nebraska Act on January 4, 1854. If passed, it would allow the citizens of Kansas and Nebraska to vote on slavery within their borders and decide for themselves whether they wanted slavery or not.

The Missouri Compromise Act, passed on March 2, 1820, to uphold the stability of control in Congress between the Slave States and the Free States, prohibited slavery in both future States of Kansas and Nebraska because the land lay North of 36° 30 (a line parallel to and contrasting to the boundary between Missouri and Arkansas), which outlawed slavery in the Louisiana territory.

CHAPTER 9

The Kansas-Nebraska Act passed on May 30, 1854, repealing the Missouri Compromise Act. While there were no debates in Nebraska because most of the state settlers were opposed to slavery, Nebraska was more to the North of the United States and not surrounded by the states which had slavery. The citizens in Nebraska already knew that the election would remain antislavery.

Many outraged antislavery settlers began to see more proslavery dwellers from different territories impact the election. More antislavery colonists moved to the region as well.

The pro-slavery citizens stood victorious in the election. Still, the antislavery citizens claimed the proslavery citizens committed voter fraud, so the antislavery citizens arranged another election that the pro-slavery citizens had no part in, which caused two conflicting governments. Then violence took a turn for the worse when both proslavery and antislavery forces led by John Brown clashed. The territory's nickname became "bleeding Kansas," with approximately 55 deaths.

Franklin Pierce reinforced the proslavery effort because of how Franklin Pierce saw it, proslavery remained a constitutional right, and he sent federal troops to end the violence.

The territory of Kansas was at a stalemate even after both parties agreed to hold another election which The proslavery citizens won again; however, the antislavery citizens claimed the proslavery citizens cheated again. After the second election, Congress got involved and ultimately agreed with the antislavery citizens and did not recognize the Constitution from the proslavery citizens.

In due course, the antislavery residents exceeded the proslavery citizens, creating a different Constitution. On January 29, 1861, close to the start of the Civil War, Kansas was declared to the Union as a free state. It became the thirty-fourth state.

Could history be a pattern of inevitable future events which date parallel in time and space?

Stephen Douglas of Illinois introduced a bill known as the Kansas-Nebraska Act on January 4, 1854. George Eacker was friends with Aaron Burr Junior before he shot Philip Hamilton. George Eacker died January 4, 1804, on Aaron Burr Senior's birthday, January 4, 1716. Aaron Burr Senior was the father of Aaron Burr Junior, who shot Alexander Hamilton. George Eacker died 50 years before Stephen Douglas introduced the Kansas/Nebraska Act.

CHAPTER 10

After the Kansas — Nebraska Act passed on May 30, 1854, major chaos escalated, and violence worsened. The territory earned the nickname Bleeding Kansas. Kansas was a lead-up to the actual American Civil War. On May 30, 1922, The Lincoln Memorial was dedicated Sixty-eight years after the Kansas/Nebraska Act agreement. The first Memorial Day in America's history was on May 30, 1868, which honors those who died in active military duty.

In due course, the Kansas/Nebraska Act's difficulty decreased, and Kansas was admitted to the Union as a free state on January 29, 1861. The same year Kansas was admitted to the Union as a free state in 1861, the same year that the Civil War began, and the same year the future twenty-fifth president William McKinley enlisted as a private in the Union Army.

When William McKinley was born on January 29, 1843, his birth became an 18-year prelude before Kansas entered the Union as a free state on January 29, 1861.

After William McKinley enlisted in the Union Army on June 11, 1861. One hundred-two years later, on June 11, 1963, the thirty-fifth president John F. Kennedy ordered integration of the University of Alabama when Governor George Wallace barred two black students, James Hood, and Vivian Malone, from entering the University. President John Kennedy sent an answer to Wallace when he called out the National Guard, Wallace then moved aside. That evening the thirty-fifth president made a primary Civil Rights televised address to the Nation. Kennedy pledged to formally ask Congress for legislation to stop segregation in all public facilities.

The Author of the Declaration of Independence, Thomas Jefferson, was born April 13, 1743. He died on July 4, 1826. Fort Sumner was the battle that ignited the Civil War on April 12, 1861. The Confederacy achieved victory after 34 hours of bombardment and artillery exchange. Eighty-six Union soldiers and the commander Robert Anderson surrendered the fort the next day, April 13, 1861, Thomas Jefferson's One-hundred-and-eighteenth birthday. Jefferson Davis's father, Samuel Davis, named his son after Thomas Jefferson. Samuel Davis died on July 4, 1824, exactly two years before Thomas Jefferson died on July 4, 1826. Jefferson Davis's vice president's name was Alexander Hamilton Stevens. Abraham Lincoln's vice president's name was Hannibal Hamlin, who died July 4, 1891.

CHAPTER 11

The very first organized battle of the Civil War was the Battle of Philippi which led to West Virginia separating from Virginia and becoming its own Union state. The Battle of Philippi came to a skirmish on June 3, 1861. It wasn't a massive battle, but it was still considered the first organized battle of the Civil War. The birth of Confederate President Jefferson Davis was the birth of the Civil War. The President of the Confederacy, Jefferson Davis, was also born on June 3, 1808. Richmond, Virginia, became the Capital of the Confederacy.

Stephen Douglas died on Jefferson Davis's birthday, June 3, 1861, the same day as the first organized battle of the Civil War, the Battle of Philippi.

Both Abraham Lincoln and Jefferson Davis were born in Kentucky.

The Battle of Perryville, the biggest battle in Kentucky, was fought on October 8, 1862. It became a Confederate victory until the Union sent reinforcements to fight General Braxton Bragg's army. In return, it became a Union victory and enforced the Union control of Kentucky for the rest of the war.

The fourteenth president, Franklin Pierce, the one who endorsed the Kansas/Nebraska Act, died on October 8, 1869. Franklin Pierce's father's name was Benjamin Pierce. Franklin died 76 years after John Hancock's passing on October 8, 1793.

Col. Peyton H. Colquitt, a Confederate officer, on September 20, 1863, during the battle of Chickamauga in Georgia, was mortally wounded and died two days later on September 22, 1863. He died exactly one year after the Preliminary Emancipation Proclamation. He was born October 8, 1831, thirty-eight years after John Hancock, who died October 8, 1793. John Hancock was the Continental President when the 56 signers signed the Declaration of Independence. John Hancock died at the age of 56 years old. Abraham Lincoln also died at the age of 56 years old.

Col. Peyton H. Colquitt was also born thirty-eight years before Franklin Pierce passed on October 8, 1869. Franklin Pierce from New Hampshire signed the Kansas/Nebraska Act, creating violence within its territory.

When Col. Peyton H. Colquitt died exactly a year after Abraham Lincoln issued the Preliminary Emancipation Proclamation, which stated that the enslaved people in all areas designated as being in rebellion as of January 1, 1863, would "be then, thenceforward, and forever free."

Thirty-eight and Thirty-eight equals seventy-six, a number indicated initially as freedom from the year of the Declaration of Independence.

"When in the course of human events it becomes necessary for one people to dissolve the political bands which have connected them with another and to assume among the powers of the earth, the separate and equal station to which the laws of nature and nature's God entitle them, a decent respect to the options of mankind requires that they should declare the causes which impel them to the separation. We hold these truths to be self—evident, that all men are created equal, that they are endowed by their Creator with certain unbillable Rights, that among these are life, liberty and the pursuit of happiness."

The thirty-eighth president, Gerald Ford, stood as the President when the United States turned two hundred years old. A woman who grew up in West Virginia, Sarah Jane Moore, failed to assassinate the thirty-eighth President Gerald Ford in San Francisco on September 22, 1975, the second attempt by a woman to assassinate Gerald Ford within seventeen days of one another. The first attempt to assassinate the thirty-eighth president was by Lynette "Squeaky" Fromme in Sacramento on September 5, 1975. One hundred and twelve years before Sarah Jane Moore failed to assassinate, an attempt on Gerold Ford's life, the death of Col. Peyton H. Colquitt, on September 22, 1863. One hundred and twelve years, they remained divided by two events on September 22, fifty-six. There were fifty-six signers of the Declaration of Independence. Thirty-eight and Thirty-eight equals seventy-six, a number indicated initially as freedom from the year of the Declaration of Independence. September 15 — 16, 1810, Hidalgo declared war on the colonial government in what has been named the Cry of Dolores—Mexico's Declaration of Independence. The Mexican War of Independence lasted from 1810 to 1821. Juan O Donoju was the last Spanish viceroy of New Spain.

Juan O. Donoju signed the Treaty of Cordoba on August 24, 1821. The Treaty of Cordoba was an agreement that accepted Mexico's sovereignty and arranged for the departure of Spanish forces from Mexico. Mexico's independence began on September 28, 1821; when Agustin de Iturbide became the first king of Mexico, and then Mexico became an independent government

Spain did not consent to Mexico's self-government for 15 years until December 28, 1836, when they signed the Santa Maria –(Calatrava Treaty)

On September 27, 1821, the Spanish withdrew their occupation from Mexico, ending the Mexican War of Independence. The war lasted from September 16, 1810, to September 27, 1821. Agustin de Iturbide, the first emperor of Mexico, was born in Valladolid on September 27, 1783. Mexico officially won independence from Spain on September 27, 1821, 38 years apart from Iturbide's birth.

Juan O Donoju died October 8, 1821. He died exactly ten years before Col. Payton H. Colquitt's birth.

Time is a chain reaction through different dimensions:

CHAPTER 12

Aaron Burr, in 1785, as a New York assemblyman, not only motioned for an amendment that called for the immediate emancipation of all individuals living in slavery, but he also presented a bill to grant women the right to vote. Aaron Burr died on September 14, 1836.

William McKinley served in the Union Army as the last Civil War veteran among the United States presidents. McKinley fought to preserve the Union, which ended involuntary servitude.

William McKinley died on September 14, 1901.

James Wilson, a Federalist and one of the Founding Fathers, was born in Scotland on September 14, 1742. He served on the US Supreme Court from 1789 to 1798 and signed the Declaration of Independence and the United States Constitution. James Wilson proposed the Three-Fifths Compromise for taxation, and it also allowed three-fifths of each southern state's slave population to be counted towards that state's overall population for representation in the US House of Representatives and the Electoral College to elect a president and vice president this compromise became part of the Electoral College system.

September 14-16, 1915, At the Woman Voters Convention, a petition of 500,000 names protested in San Francisco for women's suffrage. This event was achievable because it happened at the Panama-Pacific International

Exhibition in San Francisco and drew individuals from around the United States. At the event, Hellen Keller and her interpreter made speeches along with Theodore Roosevelt concerning women's rights to vote, and leaflets about women's suffrage fell from an airplane to help set up a better awareness of Women's rights. Then, the petition was sent to Washington, DC. When the petition finally made it to Washington, Woodrow Wilson agreed to view the half-million name petition, but Wilson's view concerning Women's suffrage was a state issue. Eventually, on May 21, 1919, James R. Mann of Illinois proposed to the House to approve women's right to vote. On June 4, 1919, the Senate approved the bill. Tennessee ratified the bill on August 18, 1920, and provided the three-fourths vote necessary to pass the 19th Amendment.

In 1901, the same year William McKinley passed away, he visited San Francisco on May 21st. Eighteen years later, on May 21st, 1919, James R. Mann, a representative from Illinois, proposed a resolution to the House to approve the Susan B. Anthony Amendment, which granted women the right to vote.

William McKinley was also shot at a World's Fair exhibition on September 6, 1901, and died on September 14, 1901.

Martin Luther King Junior entered Crozer's theological Seminary on September 14, 1948, where he studied pacifism, which means violence is unjustifiable. He advanced his ideas about non-violence as an approach to social reform.

According to an Article on the Princeton & Slavery website by Sherri Burr, The son of Aaron Burr, John Pierre Burr's Birth happened August 24, 1792, Contrary to his burial place that acknowledges his birth as August 26, 1792. Time will only tell is about the dates and how and where they were founded by each event and not solely by a birthday or a death day alone.

August 26, 1792, One hundred and twenty-eight years after. Secretary of State Bainbridge Colby signed the Nineteenth Amendment on August 26, 1920, which granted women the right to vote. Women's Equality Day on August 26 of each year. is celebrated

The twenty-eighth president, Woodrow Wilson, was the President when the Nineteenth Amendment was signed. Woodrow Wilson was a College of New Jersey student in 1875, which became Princeton University in 1896.

Woodrow Wilson also became a College of New Jersey professor in 1890. Aaron Burr graduated at sixteen years old from the College of New Jersey, where his father was a co-founder.

Woodrow Wilson's first wife, Ellen Louise Wilson, was Born on May 15, 1860, nine years later. The National Woman Suffrage Association was created on May 15, 1869, by one of its co-founders, Susan B. Anthony. Then Ellen Louise Wilson died while her husband served his first term as President, August 6, 1914, exactly 51 years before Lyndon B. Johnson signed the Voting Right Act of August 6, 1965. It made it illegal for any bigoted voting practices accepted in several southern states following the Civil War; it involved scare tactics, literacy tests, and poll taxes as necessary to vote. The administration of Woodrow Wilson created more division within America. A law was passed during Wilson's term in office, which made racial intermarriage a felony in the District of Columbia. Additionally, the Postmaster General he appointed ordered for his Washington offices to be segregated, and soon after, the Treasury and Navy followed suit and did the same.

On August 6, 1861 liberation of enslaved people in the seceded states was the first Confiscation Act, which stated that all enslaved people who fought with or worked for the Confederate military services were of no further obligation to their masters and freed.

The son of Aaron Burr, John Pierre Burr, died in Philadelphia, during the Civil War, on April 4, 1864, one-hundred-and-four years before Martin Luther King Junior's death on April 4, 1968. John Pierre Burr, half African-American, an American abolitionist, and a community leader, was born on August 24, 1792. **His birth came about precisely 22 years before the battle of Bladensburg.**

General Robert Ross led the British regiment to victory on August 24, 1814, in the Battle of Bladensburg; then, on the same night, they invaded Washington DC with 4500 men and set numerous fires at government and military buildings which also included the White House (then called the "Presidential Manson"). Afterward, The British began a sea/land operation to capture Baltimore, the third largest city in the U.S., and gained a prosperous seaport off the Chesapeake Bay.

In the Battle of Northpointe, Maryland, on September 12, Major Gen. Robert Ross was killed by a sniper before any battle even happened. Ross's replacement was by Ross's second in command, Colonel Author Brooke, who tried to advance towards Baltimore until the American Brig met him. Gen. John Strickler and his unit caused heavy casualties to the British. Strickler retreated that same day with numerous American losses as well. Brooke tried to recover from a harsh blow and decided to delay the march to Baltimore until the next day in horrible weather and rain conditions with minimal shelter. The next day, outside Baltimore, Brooke approached braced embankments and was overwhelmed by additional American militia troops. Brooke attempted to follow through with his part of the actual land/Sea operation.

But finally, he decided the Americans were too strong in Baltimore to continue.

Aaron Burr died on September 14. 1836.

His death came about 22 years after The Star-Spangled Banner was composed in Baltimore, Maryland.

In Baltimore, Maryland: Francis Scott Key was escorted by the American prisoner exchange agent Col. John Stuart Skinner to the British ship HMS "Tonnant" under Admiral Cochrane's command.

Skinner and Key were there to navigate the release of the American physician William Beanes. The British said, in short, they would honor their prisoner exchange, but it would only happen after the attack on Fort McHenry. Key, Skinner, and Beans, the ex-prisoner, were not permitted to depart because they had become aware of the British strategy of attacking the American forces. The British attack at Fort McHenry with nineteen ships, motor shells, and rocket vessel shells started at 6:30 AM on September 13. It lasted 25 hours until the following day, September 14, 1814. At dawn, Francis Scott Key saw the American flag still waving. Back in Baltimore, it inspired him to write the Star-Spangled Banner.

Aaron Burr was born on February 6, 1756.

Francis Scott Key's mother, Phoebe Penn Dagworthy, was born on the same day as Aaron Burr, February 6, 1756, came about exactly 22 years after Aaron Burr and Phoebe Penn Dagworthy were born.

In the Revolutionary War, on February 6, 1778, France and the United States of America signed the Treaty of Amity and Commerce and the Treaty of Alliance in Paris. This treaty created a military alliance against Great Britain that helped the United States achieve independence from Great Britain.

Phoebe Penn Dagworthy died July 8, 1830, exactly 54 years after July 8, 1776, when John Nixon read the Declaration of Independence to the public before the Pennsylvania State House.

The thirtieth president of the United States, Calvin Coolidge, was born July 4, 1872; 54 years later, he turned out to be President July 4, 1926, when the country turned 150 years old.

When the country turned 150 years old on July 4, 1926, Calvin Coolidge's wife, Grace Anna Goodhue Coolidge, died on July 8, 1957. She was 78 years old. The same year France and the United States signed the Treaty of Amity and Commerce in alliance against Great Britain. Following the Civil War, the Star-Spangled Banner gained an increasingly potent symbol of national unity:

"O' the land of the free and the home of the brave." The Kansas-Nebraska Act in 1854. was established.

The beginning to a very long end began in the year 54. The Kansas-Nebraska Act was a prelude to the Civil War that lasted four years and had more casualties than any other war the United States battled. Calvin Coolidge was President one hundred fifty years after the Declaration of Independence. Slavery was over, but America was still struggling with segregation. Two hundred years after the Declaration of Independence, Gerald Ford was President. His wife, Betty Ford, died on July 8, 2011. Precisely 54 years after Grace Coolidge died, July 8, 1957.

22+54 = 76—Freedom/ William Howard Taft Dedicated the Lincoln Memorial on May 30, 1922, in Washington, D.C... In 1854, the anti-slavery party, the Republican Party, was founded. Abraham Lincoln was voted the first Republican President of the United States in 1860. John Quincy Adams was President of the United States when the country turned Fifty Years old on July 4, 1826. John Quincy Adams's father, John Adams, died when his son stood as The President of The United States on July 4, 1826, the same day The United

States turned fifty years old. John Quincy Adams was part of the Democrat-Republican party when he was president; later, he switched his political affiliation to the Whig party when he was a congressman. Northern Whigs and the Southern Whigs were divided on the issue of slavery, The Whig Party fell apart after the Kansas-Nebraska Act of 1854. Northern Whigs joined the new Republican Party, while Southern Whigs joined the nativist American Party and later the Constitutional Union Party.

The Whig Party still opposed Andrew Jackson and the new Democratic Party. — Ulysses S. Grant, a Republican, was The President of The United States when the country turned a hundred- years old. Ulysses S. Grant's only daughter, Nellie Grant, was born July 4, 1855 —Calvin Coolidge, a Republican, was the President of The United States when the nation turned one hundred and fifty years old. Calvin Coolidge was born on July 4, 1872. Gerald Ford, a Republican, was the President of the United States when the Declaration of Independence turned two-hundred-year-old.

William Wilberforce, born August 24, 1759, was the essential key representative against slavery in Britain. William Wilberforce helped to start a society for proclamations society and a society for effecting the Abolition of the slave trade. On May 12, 1789, in the British Parliament, he delivered his first speech against the slave trade. On March 25, 1807, the anti-slave trade bill gave Royal Assent. Then on July 26, 1833, the Bill which abolished slavery, The Slavery Abolition Act, passed in the House of Commons. Three days later, Wilberforce died July 29, 1833. The Bill received Royal assent on August 28, 1833. Martin Luther King, I Have a Dream speech was on August 28, 1963

The Battle of Bladensburg, August 24, 1814, led to the Star-Spangled Banner, composed by Francis Scott Key, 55 years after William Wilberforce's birth.

Juan O'Donoju signed the Treaty of Cordoba on August 24, 1821, which made Mexico Independent from Spain.

CHAPTER 13

Alexander Hamilton died July 12, 1804. Theodore Roosevelt's son, Theodore Roosevelt Junior, died on July 12, 1944.

Dolly Madison, the wife of the Father of the Constitution, James Madison, died July 12, 1849, five years after Alexander Hamilton's death.

Alexander Hamilton wrote two-thirds of the Federalist Papers, which promoted a Federal Government, which listed the powers of the National Government and reserved all other powers to the states —— it covered the management of the national government by splitting it into three parts, each with an individual purpose. James Madison, Alexander Hamilton, and John Jay wrote 85 articles and essay collections.

Theodore Roosevelt Junior, at age 56, was the oldest man in the Normandy invasion at the Utah Beach landing. Theodore Roosevelt Junior died July 12, 1944, of a heart attack in France 36 days after the Invasion of D- Day.

Theodore Roosevelt Junior's youngest son Capt. Quentin Roosevelt II was among the first wave of soldiers at Omaha Beach on June 6, 1944. was named after Theodore Roosevelt Junior's youngest brother Quentin Roosevelt, who was a second lieutenant in the United States Army.

Alexander Hamilton named his last son Philip Hamilton II after his first son. Philip Hamilton died November 24, 1801, when he first encountered

George Eacker the day before in a duel. On November 24, 1963, Jack Ruby assassinated John F. Kennedy's assassin, Lee Harvey Oswald.

Quentin Roosevelt died in World War I on July 14, 1918, while behind the German line, his Aerial combat plane was hit and shot down; Gerald Ford was born in Omaha, Nebraska July 14, 1913. He was the bicentennial President, born five years before Quentin Roosevelt's passing in Aisne, France. Capt. Quentin Roosevelt II was among the first wave of soldiers at Omaha at the Battle of D-Day.

Quentin Roosevelt was born in Washington, DC, on November 19, 1897.

The Gettysburg Address November 19, 1863.

Abraham Lincoln honored the soldiers who made the ultimate sacrifice, creating a "new nation for life, liberty, and the pursuit of happiness. That all men are created equal under God." Alexander Hamilton died July 12, 1804, in the same place his son died November 24, 1801, in Weehawken, New Jersey.

Pres. Lincoln signed the Senate Joint Resolution Number—82 on July 12, 1862. The Army Medal of Honor was born. The first Army Medal of Honor was awarded to Private Jacob Parrott in 1863 for actions during the Civil War. Theodore Roosevelt Junior was awarded the Medal of Honor on September 21, 1944. His father, Theodore Roosevelt, received the Medal of Honor in 2001 and became the first president to receive the Medal of Honor. Quentin Roosevelt II also died in a plane crash on December 21, 1948.

December 26, 1776, in the Battle of Trenton, Alexander Hamilton served as an artillery captain.

CHAPTER 14

William McKinley Senior died November 24, 1892, at 85.

Phillip Hamilton, the son of Alexander Hamilton, died in a duel on November 24, 1801.

On July 4, 1850, Zachary Taylor consumed excessive raw fruit and iced milk, which caused some digestive problems. He was celebrating the 4th of July at a fund-raising event with the grandson of Martha Washington (George Washington Custis), who helped to raise funds during the construction of the Washington Monument. After the Fourth of July celebration, Taylor's health began to deteriorate. Then on July 9, 1850, he died. Zachary Taylor's doctor concluded that he died of Cholera, a small intestine bacterial infection.

Alexander Hamilton's oldest son and the youngest son were named Philip. Zachary Taylor's birthday was the same as Philip's death day. Zachary Taylor's death was on the same day as Philip II deathday. After Philip Hamilton died in a duel with George Eacker, his youngest brother, Philip II, was named after his older brother Philip.

Philip Hamilton died November 24, 1801.

Zachary Taylor was born on November 24, 1784.

Philip Hamilton II died July 9, 1884.

Zachary Taylor died July 9, 1850.

William McKinley Senior died November 24, 1892, 108 years after the 12th president, Zachary Taylor, was born November 24, 1784. Philip Hamilton II died July 9, 1884, 108 years after George Washington read the Declaration of Independence in New York on July 9, 1776.

On July 4, 1776, Congress approved a final draft of the Declaration of Independence. On July 9, 1776, the last colony, New York, approved the Declaration of Independence, and George Washington read the Declaration of Independence to his troops in New York City.

On July 4, 1850, Zachary Taylor attended the ceremony and got food poisoning, then died five days later on July 9, 1850.

On July 4, 1884, France presented the Statue of Liberty to the United States. Five days later, Philip Hamilton II died on July 9, 1884. July 4, 1776, was the first Independence Day. On July 4, 1884, France presented the Statue of Liberty to the United States, precisely 108 years apart.

The Constitution ratified the 14th Amendment on July 9, 1868. The Amendment stated that: "No state shall make or enforce any law which shall abridge the privileges or immunities of citizens of the United States, nor shall any liberty, or property, without due process of law; nor deny to any person within its jurisdiction the equal protection of the laws."

Zachary Taylor died July 9, 1850, 18 years before the 14th Amendment, July 9, 1868. was ratified.

CHAPTER 15

Theodore Roosevelt died on January 6, 1919.

Thomas Lincoln was born on January 6, 1778.

The 26th President Theodore Roosevelt died January 6, 1919, on the 16th President Abraham Lincoln's father's birthday, Thomas Lincoln, who was born January 6, 1778, exactly 141 years apart. On January 6, 1941, President Franklin Roosevelt gave his "four freedoms" speech while delivering the State of the Union address.

Franklin Roosevelt's animated image of freedom during World WW II, which were the four fundamental freedoms. Roosevelt's support for liberty against the Dictatorial Governments of Germany and Japan that tried to rule the world. Roosevelt gave his Four Freedoms speech before the U.S. entered WWII; This speech supported his vision of freedom.

First, freedom, the freedom of expression, all over the world. Religion is the second freedom, the freedom to worship God in your way universally in the world. Third, freedom and economic understanding will protect every Nation and bring its inhabitants a healthy, peaceful life. Fourth, freedom from fear and a worldwide reduction of weapons (instrument of war/weapons).

Franklin Roosevelt's wife was Eleanor Roosevelt. Eleanor Roosevelt's Father was Elliott Bulloch Roosevelt, the younger brother of the twenty-sixth president Theodore Roosevelt.

Victory in America was on August 14, 1945, when Japan first announced an unconditional surrender, ending World War II. Elliott Bulloch Roosevelt died August 14, 1894, fifty-one years later Japan surrendered. Abraham Lincoln's only Grandson, Abraham Lincoln II, was born on August 14, 1873 and died at the age of Sixteen years old of blood poisoning. Coolidge's second son, Calvin Coolidge Jr killed at Sixteen years old of blood Poisoning. Abraham Lincoln was the first U.S. Republican President. Calvin Coolidge accepted the Republican nomination for reelection on August 14, 1924, fifty-one years after Abraham Lincoln II's birth.

The 26th President Theodore Roosevelt:

"Speak softly and carry a big stick. You will go far."

When Franklin Roosevelt was serving his third term as President on December 7, 1941, The Japanese attacked Pearl Harbor. December 11, 1941, Hitler declared war on the United States.

George Washington was born on February 22, 1732.

After serving as the 6th President of the United States, John Quincy Adams served as a member of the House of Representatives, representing Massachusetts on February 21, 1848. He collapsed on the house floor due to a stroke. Adams lived one full day, February 22, on George Washington's birthday. Then he died the next day, February 23, 116 years after Washington was born in 1732.

George Washington's first inauguration as first president was on April 30, 1789. It was 40 years before the disappearance of John Quincy Adam's first son, George Washington Adams, named after George Washington. George Washington Adams disappeared on April 30, 1829, on board a steamship named after Benjamin Franklin. George Washington Adams was twenty-eight years old when he disappeared. It was a possible suicide. Adolf Hitler died on April 30, 1945, 116 years after George Washington Adam's death.

Adolf Hitler committed suicide in Berlin on April 30, 1945, at 56 years old, 156 years after Washington's inauguration.

116-40=76   116+40=156

George Washington Adams was born in Berlin, Germany, on April 12, 1801.

Franklin Roosevelt died on April 12, 1945, 144 years apart.

156-144=12 156+144=300

April 12 April 30

January 30

Franklin Delano Roosevelt was born on January 30, 1882. Fifty-one years before, Adolf Hitler was named Chancellor on January 30, 1933.

Franklin Delano Roosevelt was Fifty-one years old at his first presidential inauguration.

Franklin Delano Roosevelt died on April 12, 1945. Adolf Hitler died on April 30, 1945, 18 days apart.

Klara Hitler (Adolf Hitler's mother) died on December 21, 1907, and George Patton died on December 21, 1945. 38 years apart.

On April 12, 1776, Halifax, North Carolina, was the first to call for total Independence from Great Britain after the Patriots from North Carolina defeated the British at The Battle of Moors Creek Bridge. The Loyalists had thirty killed; nevertheless, the Patriots only suffered one loss of life... North Carolina voted in approval of Independence when they adopted the Halifax Resolves; they voted to send delegates to the Second Continental Congress to vote for Independence before the other colonies declared their Independence from Great Britain. Roger Sherman was on the committee of five that drafted the Declaration of Independence on June 28, 1776, and he was the only founding father who signed all four documents: the Articles of Association, the Declaration of Independence, the Articles of Confederation, and the United States Constitution.

On April 12th, 1776, North Carolina passed the Halifax Resolves. That same day, Mehetabel Sherman, the mother of Roger Sherman, passed away. Eighty-four years later, in 1860, Abraham Lincoln was elected the sixteenth President of the United States. The following year, on April 12th, the Civil War broke out in South Carolina, starting a long and brutal conflict. In 1944, Franklin D. Roosevelt was re-elected for his fourth presidential term. On April 12th, 1945, he passed away, precisely Eighty-four years after the start of the Civil War.

The birth of Roger Sherman was on April 19, 1721; on April 19, 1775, the first battle of the Revolutionary War, Lexington, and Concord marked the start of American Independence fifty-four years after Roger Sherman's birth. Roger Sherman died on July 23, 1793. Ulysses S. Grant became the Supreme Union General during the Civil War, the war that ended slavery. Ulysses S. Grant, who also became the 18th president of the United States, passed away on July 23, 1885, ninety-two years after Sherman's death. Ninety-two fifty-four is a thirty-eight-year gap.

CHAPTER 16

Theodore Roosevelt Senior was born on September 22, 1831. He died on February 9, 1878.

The preliminary Emancipation Proclamation, September 22, 1862, when Abraham Lincoln announced that if the rebel states did not rejoin the Union by January 1, 1863, the slaves would be freed in the rebellious states.

The Revolutionary War started after February 9, 1775, when Parliament declared Massachusetts to be in a state of rebellion which led to the first battle of the Revolutionary War. The Lexington and Concord Battle took place in Massachusetts on April 19, 1775. From the time Parliament declared Massachusetts to be in a state of rebellion on February 9, 1775, to the date that Jefferson Davis, a Senator from Mississippi, had been elected Provisional President of the Confederacy on February 9, 1861, it happened 86 years from each other. At the start of the Civil War, Major Robert Anderson, with his 86 Union Soldiers after 34 hours on an Island Fortification of Fort Sumter, surrendered the fort the following day. Lincoln then called for a militia to overthrow the rebellion.

William Henry Harrison, the 9th President, was born February 9, 1773, 36 years after Thomas Paine was born February 9, 1737. Andrew Jackson died June 8, 1845, 36 years after Thomas Paine died June 8, 1809. James Madison introduced the Bill of Rights on June 8, 1789, 20 years before Thomas Paine died on June 8, 1809.

36+20 = 56 signers of the Declaration of Independence.

In the year 1776. When Thomas Paine published his common sense pamphlet, which ignited the Declaration of Independence 36 years later, the War of 1812 began on June 18, 1812. In the War of 1812, the future seventh president Andrew Jackson and the future ninth president William Henry Harrison were Major Generals.

Winston Churchill, the prime minister of Great Britain during World War II, was born on November 30, 1874, in the United Kingdom, precisely 100 years after Thomas Paine arrived in America with a recommendation from Benjamin Franklin on November 30, 1774.

Thomas Paine was the most influential in creating the American Declaration of Independence. He published his common sense writings which transformed a nation of unaware citizens into a patriotic revolution. In the words of Patrick Henry, "Give me liberty or give me death," the same meaning in the writings of Thomas Paine. After reading Thomas Paine's common sense, the 13 colonies knew what freedom meant and why they fought for it.

Thomas Paine published an antislavery essay, African Slavery in America which he signed, Justice and Humanity, a month before he and other Philadelphian liberals set up the Society for the Relief of Free Negros Unlawfully Held in Bondage April 14, 1775, Americans first abolished group.

John Pierre Burr died on April 4, 1864, exactly a year before Abraham Lincoln and his son Tad, who had just turned 12 years old April 4, 1865, visited the devastation of the former capital of the Confederacy, Richmond, Virginia.

Martin Luther King died on April 4, 1968. Around 250,000 people gathered on August 28, 1963, to listen while Martin Luther King spoke "I Have a Dream" at the Lincoln Memorial in Washington, DC. One hundred thirty years earlier, Great Britain gave Royal assent for the Slavery Abolition Act on August 28, 1833. It took effect on August 1, 1834. It liberated enslaved people from the burden of colonies in the Caribbean in South Africa.

September 17, 1787, was the day that the 39 delegates signed the Constitution. Seventy-five years after that, on September 17, 1862, was the Battle of Antietam, the worst one-day struggle in United States history ever. Seventy-five years after that, on September 17, 1937, the face of Abraham Lincoln was the fourth presidential likeness completed on Mount Rushmore. Capt. In the Continental Militia, John Parker commanded the first Battle of the Revolutionary War at Lexington and Concord on April 19, 1775. Capt. John Parker died September 17, 1775, of Tuberculosis.

September 17, 1862, The Battle of Antietam in Sharpsburg, Maryland, was the worst one-day battle in United States history. On a day that would endure more battleground killings than any other battle day in United States history. One of the reasons why Lee wanted to March into the Northern territories of Maryland and then into Pennsylvania was that Lee wanted the Confederate Army to occupy Union territory to hopefully divide the Union Democrats from the new Republican party into the Congressional parties and conquer the North through the election process. Jefferson Davis viewed a victory at Antietam as an opportunity for Europe to recognize the Confederacy and even get on board with the Confederacy's objective. Britain and France felt an economic loss because of the Civil War in America. The Union blocked all shipments to the Confederate states. Even though barricades led into the Confederate states, the British private citizens and private companies still managed to smuggle weapons to the Confederates. Antietam's battle was crucial to the Union because Robert E Lee was unsuccessful in the Confederacy's first attempt to enter Yankee territory. The action of Antietam was the factor that led Abraham Lincoln to start the preliminary Emancipation Proclamation on September 22, 1862. The Emancipation Proclamation, which took effect on January 1, was also the factor in which the British Government denounced their original position of being neutral from a proclamation that Queen Victoria issued in 1861 to denounce the Confederacy altogether. Britain abolished slavery in 1833.

Nathan Hale, American Soldier and a Spy for the Continental Army, during the Revolutionary War, was captured by the British. Then on September

22, 1776, he was executed. Nathan Hale's last words were, as legend has it, "The only regret I have but one life to lose for my country."

Two presidents who had never enslaved people were John Adams and his son John Quincy Adams continued adamantly opposing slavery in the United States. John Quincy Adams lost the presidency in 1828 to Andrew Jackson. After John Quincy Adams served as President, he became a representative of the House of Representatives representing Massachusetts. In John Quincy Adam's last days, he had a stroke on the house floor on February 21, 1848, and died on February 23. John Quincy Adams served with Abraham Lincoln, a representative of Illinois at the time of John Quincy Adam's death. John Quincy Adams had three sons; the first after George Washington, George Washington Adams, and the second son named after John Quincy Adams' father, John Adams. And his third son Charles Francis Adams Senior. Charles Francis Adam Senior's second son was named John Quincy Adams II after Charles Adams, the old's father. John Quincy Adams II was born September 22, 1833: the Preliminary Emancipation Proclamation, September 22, 1862.

John Adams was on the committee of five that wrote the Declaration of Independence. John Adams died July 4, 1826, 50 years after the Declaration of Independence. John Adams' son, John Quincy Adams, was President when the U.S. was 50 years old. John Quincy Adams' second son, John Adams II, was born July 4, 1803, when the Author of the Declaration of Independence, Thomas Jefferson, was the third president of the United States.

The second president John Adams and the third president Thomas Jefferson died on John Adams II's 23rd birthday, a symbol for the second and third presidents. John Adams' second son Charles Adams was born on May 29, 1770. John F. Kennedy was born on May 29, 1917. Charles Adams' daughter, Abigail Louisa Smith Adams Johnson, died July 4, 1836. Precisely ten years after her grandfather's death on July 4, 1826. John Adams' wife, Abigail Adams, was born on November 22, 1744. John F. Kennedy on November 22, 1963. was assassinated.

Abraham Baldwin was born November 22, 1754, 10 years after Abigail Adams' birth. Abraham Baldwin was a founding father, an American minister, and a signer of the Constitution who represented Georgia at the Constitutional Convention. Abraham Baldwin died on March 4, 1807. On March 4, 1865, President Abraham Lincoln was inaugurated for a second term when he gave one of the best speeches he had ever made with malice towards none. Lincoln spoke of forgiveness of both North and South and for the country to unite.

Governor Morris, who believed in a strong central government, was 1 of 39 delegates that signed the Constitution. Governor Morris composed the words 'We The People in the Constitution. James Madison, who was at the convention on August 8, 1787, understood that Morris spoke directly in opposition to slavery. Morris declared it absurd to say that an enslaved person was considered a man and property. Governor Morris, who represented Pennsylvania at the Continental Convention in 1787, died November 6, 1816. On November 6, 1860, Abraham Lincoln was elected the 16th President of the United States. Jefferson Davis was voted to a six-year term as the Confederate President on November 6, 1861.

The lead-up to the Declaration of Independence started before the Continental Congress existed.

In 1765, Great Britain passed the Stamp Act, which taxed paper products like cards, printed materials, and legal documents that must bear a tax stamp. On March 18, 1766, Parliament repealed the Stamp Act. The Declaratory Act was passed on the same day the Stamp Act was repealed. The Declaratory Act meant that Parliament could pass any desired law, affecting British citizens and Colonists alike.

In 1773, led by Samuel Adams with Paul Revere and the citizens of Boston, tired of taxation without representation, dumped 342 cases of tea imported by the British into the harbor.

In retaliation to the colonists in 1773, the British Parliament passed the Intolerable Act in 1774. The Coercive Acts of 1774, known as the Intolerable Acts in the American colonies, was a series of four laws passed by the British Parliament to punish the colony of Massachusetts for the Boston Tea Party incident. One of the four laws passed was the Quartering Act, which punished occupied private homes and allowed soldiers to board occupied private dwellings. IN 1774, the first Continental Congress met in Carpenters Hall in Philadelphia from September 5 to October 26. They elected the first Continental President, Peyton Randolph, and signed the Articles of Association. Adopted On July 5, 1775, Congress sent the Olive Branch Petition to the king as a last attempt to prevent war from being declared.

In 1774, Benjamin Franklin met Thomas Paine in London. By November 30, 1774, Thomas Paine arrived in the U.S. from Great Britain with a recommendation from Benjamin Franklin. He took a position as executive editor of a new publication called Pennsylvania Magazine. Thomas Paine recognized the British order coexisted with a tyranny of aristocracy and monarchy.

On March 1775, Thomas Paine published an antislavery essay a month before April 14, 1775, when he and other Philadelphia liberals established the Society for the Relief of Free African-Americans unlawfully held in bondage, America's first abolished group, which was 90 years before Lincoln was shot on April 14, 1865, by John Booth.

On January 9, 1776, Thomas Paine published Common Sense leading to the Declaration of Independence. It explained why America fought Great Britain and why freedom was worth dying for.

On June 7, 1776, Richard Henry Lee introduced a motion declaring independence to the second Continental Congress. On June 11, the Second Continental Congress appointed a committee of five to draft the Declaration of Independence. On June 28, 1776, The committee of five sent the final draft to the Continental Congress. Then, on July 2, Congress voted for independence. On July 4, Congress approved the Final Draft, and independence was then declared.

To Americans: African Slavery in America-

That some desperate wretches should be willing to steal and enslave men by violence and murder for gain is more lamentable than strange. But that many civilized, nay, Christianized people should approve and be concerned in the savage practice is surprising and persists. However, it has often been proved contrary to the light of nature, to every principle of Justice and Humanity, and even good policy, by a succession of eminent men and several late publications. Our Traders in MEN (an unnatural commodity!) must know the wickedness of the SLAVE-TRADE if they attend to reasoning or the dictates of their hearts and shun and stifle all these, willfully sacrificing Conscience and the character of integrity to that golden idol. The Managers of the Trade themselves and others testify that many of these African nations inhabit fertile countries, are industrious farmers, enjoy plenty, and lived quietly, averse to war before the Europeans debauched them with liquors and bribed them against one another, and that these inoffensive people are brought into slavery, by stealing them, tempting Kings to sell subjects, which they can have no right to do, and hiring one tribe to war against another, to catch prisoners. By such wicked and inhuman ways, the English are said to enslave towards one hundred thousand yearly, of which thirty thousand are supposed to die by barbarous treatment in the first year; besides, all that are slain in the unnatural ways excited to take them. So much innocent blood have the managers and supporters of this inhuman trade to answer for to the common Lord of all. Many of these were not prisoners of war and redeemed from savage conquerors, as some plead, and they who were such prisoners, the English, who promote the war for that very end, are the guilty authors of their being so. If they were redeemed, as is alleged, they would owe nothing to the redeemer but what he paid for them. They show as little reason as conscience who put the matter by saying — "Men, in some cases, are lawfully made slaves, and why may not these?" So, men, in some cases, are lawfully put to death, deprived of their goods, without their consent; may any man, therefore, be treated so, without any conviction of desert? Nor is this plea amended by adding — "They are set forth to us as slaves, and we buy them without further inquiry; let the sellers see to it." Such man may as well join with a known band of robbers, buy their ill-got goods, and help on the trade; ignorance is no more pleadable in one case than the other; the sellers own how they obtain them. But none can lawfully buy without evidence that they are not concurring with Men-Stealers, and as the true owner has a right to reclaim his goods that were stolen and sold, so the slave, who is the proper owner of his freedom, has a right to reclaim it, however often sold.

Most shocking is alleging the sacred scriptures to favor this wicked practice. One would have thought none but infidel cavilers would endeavor to make them appear contrary to the plain dictates of natural light and the conscience in a matter of common Justice and Humanity, which they cannot be. Such worthy men, as referred to before, judged others; Mr. Baxter declared that the slave traders should be called Devils rather than Christians and that it is a heinous crime to buy them. But some say, "the practice was permitted to the Jews." To which may be replied?

1. The example of the Jews, in many things, may not be imitated by us; they had not only orders to cut off several nations altogether, but if they were obliged to war with others and conquered them, to cut off every male; they were suffered to use polygamy and divorces, and other things utterly unlawful to us under clearer light.

2. The plea is, in a great measure, false; they had no permission to catch and enslave people who never injured them.

3. Such arguments will become us since the time of reformation came under the Gospel light. All distinctions of nations and privileges of one above other are ceased; Christians are taught to account all men their neighbors and love their neighbors as themselves, and do to all men as they would be done by; to do good to all men; and Man-stealing is ranked with enormous crimes. Is the barbarous enslaving our inoffensive neighbors and treating them like wild beasts subdued by force reconcilable with the Divine precepts? Is this doing to them as we would desire, they should do to us? If they could carry off and enslave some thousands of us, would we think it just? — One would almost wish they could for once; it might convince more than reason or the Bible.

As much in vain will they search ancient history for examples of the modern slave trade? Too many nations enslaved the prisoners they took in war. But to go to nations with whom there is no war, who have no way provoked, without the further design of conquest, purely to catch inoffensive people, like wild beasts, for slaves, is a height of outrage against humanity and justice, that seems left by heathen nations to be practiced by pretended Christian. How shameful are all attempts to color and excuse it?

As these people are not convicted of giving up freedom, they still have a natural, perfect right to it, and the governments, whenever they come, should, in justice, set them free and punish those who hold them in slavery.

So monstrous is the making and keeping them slaves at all, abstracted from the barbarous usage they suffer, and the many evils attending the practice, as selling husbands away from wives, children from parents, and each other, in violation of sacred and natural ties; and opening the way for adulteries, invests, and many shocking consequences, for all of which the guilty Masters must answer to the final Judge.

If the slavery of the parents is unjust, much more is their children's; if the parents were just slaves, yet the children are born free, this is the natural, perfect right of all mankind; they are nothing but a just recompense to those who bring them up: And as much less is commonly spent on them than others, they have a right, in justice, to be proportionably sooner free.

Certainly, one may, with as much reason and decency, plead for murder, robbery, lewdness, and barbarity as for this practice. They are not more contrary to the natural dictates of conscience and feeling of humanity; nay, they are all comprehended in it.

But the chief design of this paper is not to disprove it, which many have sufficiently done, but to entreat Americans to consider.

1. With what consistency or decency do they complain so loudly of attempts to enslave them? At the same time, they hold so many hundred thousand in slavery and annually enslave many thousands more without any pretense of authority or claim upon them.

2. How just and suitable to our crime is the punishment with which Providence threatens us? We have enslaved multitudes and shed much innocent blood in doing it, and now we are threatened with the same. And while other evils are confessed and bewailed, why not this especially, and publicity; than which no other vice, if all others, has brought so much guilt on the land?

3. Should we not all stop and renounce it immediately, with grief and abhorrence? Should not every society bear testimony against it and account

obstinate mersisters in it bad men, enemies to their country, and exclude them from fellowship, as they often do for much lesser faults?

4. The great Question may be — What should be done with enslaved people? To turn the old and infirm free would-be injustice and cruelty; they who enjoyed the labors of their better days should keep and treat them humanely. As to the rest, let prudent men, with the assistance of legislatures, determine what is practicable for masters and best for them. Perhaps some could give them lands upon reasonable rent, some, employing them in their labor still, might give them some reasonable allowances for it; so as all may have some property and fruits of their labors at their disposal and be encouraged to industry, the family may live together, and enjoy the natural satisfaction of exercising relative affections and duties, with civil protection, and other advantages, like fellow men. Perhaps they might sometimes form useful barrier settlements on the frontiers. Thus, they may become interested in the public welfare and help promote it instead of being dangerous, as they are, should any enemy promise them a better condition.

5. The past treatment of Africans must naturally fill them with abhorrence of Christians, leading them to think our religion would make them more inhuman savages if they embraced it; thus, the gain of that trade has been pursued in opposition to the redeemer's cause, and the happiness of men. Are we not, therefore, bound in duty to him and to them to repair these injuries, as far as possible, by taking some proper measure to instruct not only the slaves here but the Africans in their own countries? Primitive Christians labored always to spread the divine religion, and this is equally our duty while there is a heathen nation. But what are singular obligations? These are the principles of justice and humanity.

CHAPTER 17

James Monroe 1820 Elected Warren G. Harding 1920 Re-elected.

James Monroe died on July 4, 1831, 55 years after the Declaration of Independence on July 4, 1776. Warren G. Harding was elected President on November 2, 1920, on his 55th birthday. He was born on November 2, 1865. Warren G Harding died on August 2, 1923. Most of the Declaration of Independence signers signed on August 2, 1776— 147 years apart.

Warren G Harding's Vice President Calvin Coolidge was born on July 4, 1872. After Harding passed away while in office, Coolidge became the President of the United States. Coolidge was the President when the country turned 150 years old.

Daniel T. Tompkins was the Governor of New York before he became the Vice President of the United States under James Monroe. As Governor of New York, Tompkins proposed the emancipation of all enslaved people in New York. The act was passed on March 31, 1817, and went into effect on July 4, 1827. On March 31, 1870, Thomas Mundy Peterson became the first African American man to vote in a United States election in the State of New Jersey. On July 4, 1799, Gov. John Jay signed into law an act to gradually abolish slavery in New York. The law said that children born after July 4, 1799, to mothers who were enslaved in New York, would be born free but would have to deliver free assistance to their mothers' masters. A female until she was 25 years of age and a male at the age of 28. the law affected only those born after 1799. George Washington appointed John Jay as the first Chief Justice of the United States in 1789.

James Monroe was born on April 28, 1758, 30 years before Maryland approved the Constitution. Maryland ratified the Constitution on April 28, 1788, making it the seventh state to ratify. Calvin Coolidge was the 30th president of the United States.

Daniel T. Tompkins was born June 21, 1774, and The Constitution became law when nine of the 13 states ratified it; New Hampshire became the ninth state to ratify on June 21, 1788. Thenceforth, in due course, made the Constitution the supreme law of the United States.

Daniel T. Tompkins died June 11, 1825. On June 11, 1776, the Continental Congress appointed a committee of five to draft the Declaration of Independence: Thomas Jefferson, John Adams, Benjamin Franklin, Roger Sherman, and Robert Livingston to edit the draft. On July 4, 1776, the Declaration of Independence's final draft was permitted and approved. Independence declared!!!

Richard Henry Lee proposed independence in the Second Constitutional Congress on June 7, 1776. Richard Henry Lee was born on January 20, 1732, and died on June 19, 1794. Juneteenth is a federal holiday in the United States because on June 19, 1865, Union Soldiers reached Galveston, Texas, with information that the Civil War had ended and slavery in the United States had finally ended.

John F Kennedy's statement to Congress on June 11, 1963, followed by a bill to Congress on June 19, to emphasize the danger of segregation and racial hostilities that enacted an immoral intrusion in America. John F. Kennedy vowed to ask Congress to end segregation in America which became the civil rights act. The Bill was signed into law on July 2, 1964, by Lynden B Johnson.

Sarah Lincoln Grigsby, Abraham Lincoln's only sister, died on January 20, 1828. The 20th Amendment to the Constitution states that the President and Vice President administration will end at noon on January 20 every four years.

The United States turned 150 years old on Coolidge's 54th birthday. After battling for the abolishment of slavery for 25 years, William Lloyd Garrison understood the Nation had been deceitful since the beginning. Arriving at a big gathering on July 4, 1854, in Massachusetts, he scorched a duplicate of the Constitution and the fugitive slave act. William Lloyd Garrison was a journalist who helped open a victorious abolished crusade against slavery in the United States.

George Washington at the Battle of Dorchester Heights, which began on March 4, 1776 making the British leave Boston within weeks. In 1773, in Boston, Samuel Adams, with Paul Revere, tired of taxation without representation, dumped 342 cases of tea imported by the British into the harbor. Forty-one years after Dorchester Heights. James Monroe's first inauguration as President was on March 4, 1817.

On December 26, 1776, George Washington crossed the Delaware with James Monroe, who survived being shot and wounded in his left shoulder at the Battle of Trenton.

James Monroe died July 4, 1831, 41 years before Calvin Coolidge was born July 4, 1872. Calvin Coolidge was President when the United States turned one hundred and fifty years old on July 4, 1926. On July 4, 1776, the Founding Fathers adopted The Declaration of Independence. Thomas Jefferson, the Author, and John Adams, one of the Coauthors, died exactly 50 years after The Declaration of Independence was Adopted. James Monroe died exactly five years after John Adams and Thomas Jefferson. Thomas Jefferson was the first president that got elected on a zero year. James Monroe was the second to get elected on a zero year. On March 4, 1841, William Henry Harrison inaugurated the ninth President. Harrison was the third to get elected on the zero years and the first to die in office when the year he was elected ended with zero.

Warren G Harding died on August 2, 1923. Most of the Declaration of Independence signers signed on August 2, 1776— 147 years apart. Warren G Harding was born on November 2, 1865: James Knox Polk, The 11th president born on November 2, 1795. James Knox Polk was president during the Mexican-American war in 1847. Abraham Lincoln and John Quincy Adams served in the House of Representatives together in 1847.

Thomas Paine's Common Sense pamphlet is 47 pages.

CHAPTER 18

William Henry Harrison, 1840 Elected President

Franklin Roosevelt, 1940 Re-elected President

The ninth president, William Henry Harrison, who died on April 4, 1841, was the first to pass on the zero factor. William Henry Harrison got elected in 1840. Then he only served 32 days as President. Then he died. His father, Benjamin Harrison V, from Charles City County, Virginia, served as Virginia's fifth governor from 1781 to 1784. He was also 1 of 56 Signers of the Declaration of Independence 1776. Benjamin Harrison V died on April 24, 1791. William Henry Harrison died on April 4, 1841. Fifty years and 20 days after his father's death, Thomas Jefferson and John Adams died July 4, 1826, 50 years after the Declaration of Independence in 1776. These 20 days symbolize 20 years for every President elected on the zero factor. William Henry Harrison was elected in 1840 and died on April 4, 1841.

Benjamin Harrison V was born on April 5, 1726. William Henry Harrison died on April 4, 1841, one hundred and fifteen years and one day after his father's birth. Benjamin Harrison V was born in 1726, fifty years before 1776, and died in 1791 Fifteen years after 1776—one hundred and fifteen years after the year Benjamin Harrison V signed the Declaration of Independence in 1776, Benjamin Harrison, the great-grandson of Benjamin Harrison V, stood as the 23rd President of United States in 1891.

Fifteen years after the deaths of the Authors of the Declaration of Independence, Thomas Jefferson and John Adams, in 1826, William Henry Harrison became the ninth President of the United States in 1841. Sadly, he passed away in that same year. One hundred and fifteen years after the deaths of Jefferson and Adams, Franklin D. Roosevelt was inaugurated for his third term as President in 1941. It was also the same year that the United States entered World War II.

William Henry Harrison as president?

When William Henry Harrison gave his Inaugural Speech in Washington, DC, the temperature was a blistering 48 degrees, and he chose not to wear protection from the brutal weather. He went without gloves, no hat, and he was not even wearing an overcoat, yet it took him an hour and 45 minutes to deliver the longest inauguration speech in history, an 8445-word speech, in the cold.

William Henry Harrison was the 9th president and shortest-term president in history. He was elected in 1840 and served only 32 days before he died of pneumonia. Harrison was a major general in the Battle of Tippecanoe on November 7, 1811.

The longest-term president in history was the 32nd President Franklin Roosevelt, he was first elected in 1932. The United States entered World War II after Franklin Roosevelt's election to his third term in 1940. He was elected to a fourth term on November 7, 1944, and died in 1945.

The Battle of Tippecanoe was on November 7, 1811, in Battleground, Indiana. On November 6, Harrison, with about 1000 men near Prophetstown, prepared to meet with Tenskwatawa the following morning. On November 7, 1811, the Prophetstown Indians assaulted Harrison's army.

Harrison's men fought back for about three hours against the Prophetstown Indians. Eventually, the Indians had to flee because their ammunition ran low. Harrison burnt Prophetstown and ravaged their food supply. Afterward, they headed back home. Sixty-two of Harrison's men died.

Franklin Roosevelt's wife, Eleanor, died of aplastic anemia on November 7, 1962. She died Exactly 18 years after her husband`s reelection to his fourth and final term on November 7, 1944. He died while he was in office on April 12, 1945.

Ulysses S. Grant was the 18th President of the United States who fought in his first battle of the Civil War as a Brigadier General, on November 7, 1861, at the battle of Belmont. With nearly 3000 Union troops from the Mississippi River in Illinois, the general marched close to 3 miles to Belmont, Missouri, and attacked the Confederate grip at Fort Johnson. But Grant was forced to flee when extra Confederate troops got there. Grant and the Union army had 120 deaths in this battle.

Ulysses S. Grant in his first Civil War battle at the Battle of Belmont, November 7, 1861, to William Henry Harrison when he was a major general in the battle of Tippecanoe, November 7, 1811. 50 years

Andrew Jackson, with 4000 infantry, men November 7, 1814, clashed with the British and Spanish Soldiers at the Battle of Pensacola, Florida. On November 9, the 4000 American forces caused the British troops to withdraw from the action, ending in a Spanish surrender. Andrew Jackson was elected the seventh president in 1828 and in 1832. Reelected

Ulysses S. Grant, in his first battle of the Civil War at the Battle of Belmont November 7, 1861, to Andrew Jackson at the Battle of Pensacola November 7, 1814, 47 years apart, Belmont and Pensacola. —

At the beginning of 1847, in the Mexican-American War, Zachary Taylor and his men were vastly outnumbered in the Battle of Buena Vista against General Antonio Lopez de Santa Anna, with at least 15,000 soldiers to Zachary Taylor's 5000. Nevertheless, Taylor still arose victorious after Antonio's army retreated that night. Zachary Taylor, a war hero of the Mexican-American war, was elected the 12 president on November 7, 1848.

Franklin Roosevelt was born on January 30, 1882, to Andrew Jackson's attempted assassination on January 30, 1835, a 47-year difference. On January 30, 1835, a 32-year-old Richard Lawrence pointed a bayonet at Andrew Jackson. It misfired. He pulled out a different gun which also failed. Lawrence was found to be insane and died in an institution.

On February 15, 1933, a 32-year-old Joseph Zangard fired at the 32nd President Franklin Roosevelt in Miami, Florida, before a parade proceeded. Chicago Mayor Anton Cermak died March 6, 1933, when the bullet hit him instead.

Gen. John A. Logan founded Declaration Day on May 30, 1868. John Alexander Logan was born February 9, 1826, in Murphysboro, Illinois.

Memorial Day was initially known as Decoration Day when America honored and decorated the graves of the soldiers who died in the civil war. Today Memorial Day honors all American Soldiers who died defending the Nation.

William Henry Harrison was born February 9, 1773, and was the third president elected on a 0 year and the first president to die on the zero factors, which was after Thomas Jefferson and James Monroe, were the first two presidents elected on a zero year and they both died July 4th and five years apart.

John Logan of Illinois was a lawyer, a Democrat, and in the Illinois state legislature. John Alexander Logan was born February 9, 1826, 53 years apart from William Henry Harrison's birth. In 1853, Logan proposed a bill that passed to prevent free Blacks from traveling to Illinois. Known as "Logan's black law," it implemented a $50 fine for newcomers who stayed in Illinois for more than ten days. If they could not pay, they would be Indentured Servants by auction. Logan viewed proslavery as conventional and supported a bill to preclude Blacks from having the right to testify in court. Logan was voted to the US House In 1858. He was a Representative of the Democrat Party from Illinois in the 9th Congressional District and ran again in 1860 and won reelection.

Before John Alexander Logan resigned his seat, he served as a Col. under Ulysses S. Grant at the battle of Belmont on November 7, 1861. He also served in many other conflicts, including the battle of Fort Donelson, where he was shot through his shoulder and right thigh. He eventually became a brigadier general and then a Major General. William T. Sherman replaced him as corps commander because of his history as a politician. However, Logan still served with merit until July 13, 1865, when he returned to his previous policymaking duties. However, when he returned with a new vision. Logan returned as a Republican and advocated for African-American constitutional rights, including voting rights. He won the US elections of 1866, 1868, and 1870. Logan served as the succeeding leader of the Grand Army, where he nationalized provincial grave decorating ceremonies.

Decoration Day began right after the Civil War ended in 1868 when individuals laid flowers on Union and Confederate grave sites to honor the soldiers who lost their lives while fighting in the Civil War. Decoration Day gets more significant to keep those who have died in all American wars after World War 1. Decoration Day became Memorial Day in 1967. Then Congress passed the Uniform Monday Holiday Act in 1968, making Memorial Day observances on the last Monday in May. The law took effect in 1971. John Alexander Logan, the founder of Memorial Day, died December 26, 1886, in Washington, DC.

The thirty-third president Harry S Truman died December 26, 1972, 86 years after John Alexander Logan, who died in 86

Truman prohibited segregation from the Armed Forces on July 26, 1948, by executive order, from the President of the United States Harry S Truman "It is hereby declared to be the policy of the president that there shall be equality of treatment and opportunity for all persons in the armed services without regard to race, color, religion or national origin. This policy shall be put into effect as rapidly as possible, having due regard to the time required to effectuate any necessary changes without impairing efficiency or morale."

Fifteen years after Truman signed his executive order on July 26, 1948, Defense Secretary Robert McNamara instructed military superiors on July 26, 1963, to boycott private services that discriminated against black people used by soldiers or their families.

Then in Britain, on July 26, 1833, the bill which abolished slavery, The Slavery Abolition Act, passed in the House of Commons. Truman prohibited segregation from the Armed Forces on July 26, 1948, one hundred fifteen years after the Slavery Abolition Act.

CHAPTER 19

John F. Kennedy in 1960. Elected president

Abraham Lincoln in 1860. Elected president

President George Washington signed the Fugitive Slave Act on February 12, 1793, when a runaway slave was caught by their slaveholder. It permitted the slaveholder to hold the outlawed enslaved person and authorize them to present written official orders to recover their property.

The 16th President, Abraham Lincoln, was born on February 12, 1809. The Fugitive Slave Act was signed into law by George Washington sixteen years before the sixteenth President, Abraham Lincoln's birth.

December 14, 1863, James Ashley proposed the 13th amendment to the Constitution, which abolished slavery, precisely sixty-four years after George Washington died on December 14, 1799.

William McKinley's oldest daughter Katherine McKinley died on June 25, 1875. Exactly one year before the battle of Little big bullhorn, Gen. George Custer died June 25, 1876, close to the little big horn River in the Montana territory.

William McKinley was the president on October 18, 1898, when US troops raised the US flag over Puerto Rico in the Spanish-American war, consecrating US control of the former Spanish colony 39 years before. John

Brown's men arrived at Harper's Ferry in Virginia to start a slave rebellion. He was captured on October 18, 1859, by Robert E. Lee's soldiers. Two months later, they executed him on December 2. Eighty years after John Brown`s capture, John F. Kennedy's assassin, Lee Harvey Oswald, was born on October 18, 1939. Boston Corbett killed Abraham Lincoln's assassin, John Wilkes Booth. Boston Corbett was born on January 29, 1832. The 25th President, William McKinley, was born on January 29, 1843, 11 years apart.

The year 98 to the year 59= 39.

39+11 = 50 — Lee Harvey Oswald was born on Oct 18, 1939. Jack Ruby used March 25, 1911, as his birth.

Exactly 63 years before John Wilkes Booth was born, on May 10, 1838, the rebels proclaimed their first offensive victory of the Revolutionary War: The Battle of Fort Ticonderoga in New York. Fort Ticonderoga was a real morale booster for the Continental Army. The Green Mountain boys, under Ethan Allen and Benedict Arnold, made a surprise attack on the morning of May 10, 1775, and defeated the British.

Confederate president Jefferson Davis was captured on May 10, 1865, on John Wilkes Booth's 27th birthday 63+27 = 90. Ninety years after April 14, 1775, the Society for the Relief of Free African-Americans began; John Wilkes Booth shot Abraham Lincoln on April 14, 1865.

Lee Harvey Oswald was born on October 18, 1939. During the siege of Yorktown and the end of the Revolutionary War, the terms of surrender were completed at Moore's house on October 18, 1781. The next day, second-in-command Benjamin Lincoln, after the British surrendered, George Washington appointed Major General Lincoln to accept O'Hara's sword. Benjamin Lincoln then directed the British troops to lay down their weapons.

Benjamin Lincoln died May 9, 1810. Ten years before Benjamin Lincoln's death, John Brown, the Abolitionist, was born on May 9, 1800. Andrew Johnson, Lincoln's successor, on May 9, 1865, declared the civil war "virtually over." All events considered led to Andrew Johnson's declaration. IN VIRGINIA, Robert E. Lee surrendered to Ulysses S. Grant on April 9, 1865. Confederate General Joseph E. Johnston surrendered the Armies to William T. Sherman in North

Carolina on April 26, 1865, when The Departments of Florida, South Carolina, and South Georgia acknowledged Johnson's command. On May 4, the Confederate Department of Alabama, Mississippi, and East Louisiana surrendered to the Union. On the same day, Confederate President Jefferson Davis arranged one last cabinet meeting, and then the Confederate Government became nonexistent. The day after Andrew Johnson's declaration, The Union captured Jefferson Davis. The final Battle of the Civil War, The Battle of Palmito Ranch, Texas, was on May 13, 1865, only four days after the declaration.

Andrew Johnson's declaration was 55 years after Benjamin Lincoln's death.

Abraham Lincoln died on April 15, 1865. Congress approved the Preliminary Articles of Peace, ending the Revolutionary War with Great Britain on April 15, 1783.

The Treaty of Paris, signed by Benjamin Franklin, John Adams, and John Jay in Paris, officially concluded the American Revolutionary War. It recognized America as an Independent country on September 3, 1783. Fredrick Douglass became one of the most recognized thinkers of his time. His leadership for the abolitionist movement became a giant step forward from his life as an enslaved person. He escaped on September 3, 1838, fifty-five years after the Treaty of Paris.

The first known enslaved people from Angola lived in the first English colony of Virginia who came by a privateer ship, The White Lion, on August 20, 1619—initially kidnapped by the Portuguese on a boat that sailed from the harbor of Luanda, today`s Capital of Angola, on the way to Veracruz in the Colony of New Spain when the White Lion attacked the Portuguese ship. The private boat took the Angolans from the Portuguese, sailed to the New World, and landed on Point Comfort. When they traded the twenty Angolans for food, Jamestown originated in 1607. The American Civil War ended on August 20, 1866. As declared by Andrew Johnson, Jack Ruby assassinated Lee Harvey Oswald on November 24, 1963, precisely 100 years before November 24, 1863, Gen. Joseph Hooker in Chattanooga, Tennessee, the Union Army defeated Major General Carter L. Stevenson of the Confederacy at the Battle of Lookout Mountain.

The Confederate Army won the last Civil War battle on May 13, 1865, at Palmito Ranch, Texas. Then a month later, the Confederacy surrendered their remaining forces to the Union. On May 13, 1888, Brazil signed the Lei Aurea, known as the Golden Law, an article with only 18 words that ended slavery in Brazil. Princess Isabel of Brazil signed it. During the Atlantic Slave Trade, Brazil imported more enslaved Africans than any other nation. Brazil was also the last American Nation to put an end to slavery.

April 26, 1865, Joseph E. Johnson was the commander of the last Major Confederate Army Battle when he surrendered to William Sherman at Bennett's place. On the same day, Boston Corbett killed John Wilkes Booth on April 26, 1865. When Sherman died on February 14, 1891, someone asked Johnston to be one of his pallbearers. Johnston walked in a single file beside his former opponent's casket with no hat, not even considering the cold rain falling on his head. "If I were in his place, and he was standing here in mine, he would not put on his hat," Johnson said. Johnston caught pneumonia and died on March 21, 1891.

Britain's King George III signed into law the Slave Trade Act of March 25, 1807. The Slave Trade Act did not abolish slavery from Britain, but it made it Illegal to trade worldwide. Jack Ruby was born on March 25, 1911.

Jack Ruby died on January 3, 1967. 190 years apart. George Washington defeated the British forces in the Revolutionary War during The Battle of Princeton on January 3, 1777.

John Joseph Pershing became the highest-ranked general in US history when his rank became General of the Armies in 1919. Pershing, while he was still active in the military, came to be equivalent to a six-star General, the highest-ranked general to ever serve while in the military. George Washington was the only other Military officer to achieve this rank when the 38th President Gerald Ford signed a bill in 1976. In 1885 John Joseph Pershing became one of the original white officers to command an African-American Regiment in the 10th Cavalry. He was born September 13, 1860, and died July 15, 1948.

Abraham Lincoln's youngest son Tad Lincoln died July 15, 1871, and was born April 4, 1853. Martin Luther King died on April 4, 1968. Martin Luther

King visited the Berlin Wall on September 13, 1964. John Joseph Pershing was born September 13, 1860, 104 years before Martin Luther King spoke at the Berlin Wall. John F. Kennedy visited the Berlin Wall on June 26, 1963. Abraham Lincoln, on June 26, 1857, reacted to the unethical Dred Scott decision from the Supreme Court, which declared that Dred Scott, who lived in the Free State of Illinois and then the Free Territory of Wisconsin, did not entitle Dred Scott to his freedom after he moved back to the Slave State of Missouri.

Martin Luther King said: when he visited the Berlin Wall. "There is no East, no West... No North, no South, but one great fellowship of love worldwide."

The bloodiest one-day Battle of the Civil War was the Battle of Antietam on September 17, 1862. The Battle of Antietam led to the Preliminary Emancipation Proclamation on September 22, 1862. Thirty-nine Signers signed the Constitution on September 17, 1787. The President of the Continental Congress, George Washington, died on December 14, 1799. James Ashley proposed the 13th Amendment to the Constitution on December 14, 1863; the 13th Amendment is the Amendment that abolished slavery in the Constitution. Dred Scott died September 17, 1858.

Patrick Henry said, "Give me liberty or death," on March 23, 1775.

Patrick Henry was born May 29, 1736, and died June 6, 1799. John F Kennedy was born on May 29, 1917, and died on November 22, 1963. Robert F. Kennedy died on June 6, 1968. D-Day took place on June 6, 1944. John Adam's second son, Charles Adams, was born on May 29, 1770. John Adams' wife, Abigail Adams, was born on November 22, 1744. John Adams and his son John Quincy Adams of the first twelve presidents, were the only two presidents that never enslaved people.

Abraham Lincoln's lost speech.

They first assumed Abraham Lincoln's speech was lost forever when Abraham Lincoln spoke at the Republican State Convention of Illinois at Bloomington on May 29, 1856. Initially believed that no reporters reported this speech because the address regarding slavery was exceptionally compelling. Mr. H. C. Whitney, at that time a young lawyer in Illinois, made notes of Abraham Lincoln's speech, which he well-maintained; and after a spread of forty years, the letters finally copied and were published in the "McClure's Magazine" September 1896

From John F. Kennedy's birth May 29, 1917, to Abraham Lincoln's lost speech May 29, 1856, was exactly 61 years apart. Abraham Lincoln and John F Kennedy were both inaugurated in the year 61.

CHAPTER 20

James Garfield 1880 Ronald Regan 1980 Elecet

George Washington presided as the Constitutional Congress's President before becoming the United States' first president. George Washington and James Madison were two presidents recognized for their responsibilities in the birth of the United States Constitution. On September 17, 1787, when 39 delegates signed the Constitution. James Madison, the Father of the Constitution, wrote the document that formed the Constitution. Then on June 8, 1789, he presented the Bill of Rights to the House of Representatives and introduced the Bill of Rights in the Constitution.

Thomas Hickey was a Continental prisoner for handing out counterfeit money. When he was in prison, a plot to assassinate George Washington. was discovered.

Even though Thomas Hickey was involved with a governor and a mayor, he was still the only one who received punishment; Hickey had been found guilty of mutiny: sedition and treason. On June 28, 1776, in Manhattan, Hickey was hanged in New York City. On the same day, the final document of the Declaration of Independence was drafted in Philadelphia, 60 years before the Father of the

Constitution, James Madison, passed away on June 28, 1836, as the last surviving founding father of the United States.

There were thirty-nine signers of the Constitution. Ronald Reagan was the 40th Commander in Chief even though he was the 39th person because Grover Cleveland served two non- consecutive terms as president. He served as the 22nd and the 24th president. Grover Cleveland's wife, Frances, was born exactly three years after the first full-blown Civil War battle, the first battle of Bull Run, in Virginia on July 21, 1861. Several people assumed capturing the Confederate capital at Richmond, Virginia, would come easy because their Capital lay one hundred miles south of Washington. However, the General in Chief, Lt. Gen. Winfield Scott, thought differently. He organized a plan to conquer the Confederate States; the Union army would fight the Confederate army in the western lands, and then the U.S. Navy would block the Southern ports down the eastern and Gulf coasts, an act Lincoln previously demanded. Then, an army of 80,000 men would navigate down the Mississippi Stream and capture the biggest city in the south, New Orleans, squeeze the Confederate States out of their territory by dividing the states in half and financially, suffocate their resources by cutting the Confederacy in half and calling it the "Anaconda Plan. The newspapers scorned the" Anaconda Plan. Many people thought taking the Confederate capital would be much easier. Winfield Scott was already 75 years old and in poor physical shape, and his plan appeared unessential since the Confederate Capital was so close. Irvin McDowell spent most of his career doing staff duties before he replaced Winfield Scott, but McDowell's strategy to defeat the Confederate Army at Bull Run canceled Winfield Scott's plan. McDowell handled preparing 35,000 untrained Union volunteers, and he pushed for a suspension to give his men the right kind of training. However, President Lincoln did not want any delays. And the Union did not sufficiently train its forces. Gen. McDowell's campaign was to capture the Confederate Capital of Richmond, Virginia. Brig. Gen. P.G.T. Beauregard's Rebel Army had the same problem as the Union. The Confederate Army trained as insufficiently as the Union Army. Still, at some point in the battle, the Confederacy cracked the Union's right flank and sent the Ill-trained

Union volunteers into a disorganized retreat, which granted the Confederacy victory… Exactly two hundred and five years before the first battle of Bull Run, Elizabeth Key became the first woman of African origin to win her freedom in the thirteen colonies from a Virginia court on July 21, 1656. An English white planter was her father, and her mother was an enslaved African woman. She argued that a child follows the father's race under English law. She also claimed that under English law, a Christian cannot be enslaved either. Her case for freedom also claimed she was in indentured servitude for ten years longer than she was supposed to be. Elizabeth Key was an indentured servant under John Mottram. After John Mottram died in 1655, his heir changed Elizabeth Key's indentured servitude to an enslaved person. Elizabeth Key knew a man named William Grinstead because William Grinstead became one of many English indentured servants that John Mottram bought in 1650. When William Grinstead became a free man, He studied law and helped Elizabeth Key`s case in court, which she lost. However, she petitioned a General Assembly. A committee found Elizabeth Key within the law. Elizabeth Key won her freedom in a lower court with the committee's founding. In 1667, the Virginia legislative body passed new laws declaring baptisms did not entitle one's freedom.

Frances Cleveland died on October 29, 1947, eighty-five years after the Battle of Island Mound in Bates County, Missouri, on October 29, 1862. The Battle of Island Mound marks the first time an African-American regiment went to combat in the American Civil War. Grover Cleveland paid 32-year-old George Benninsky to take his place when the Union Army drafted Cleveland to fight in the Civil War, Benninsky was born in Poland in 1832 to take his place Benninsky had one hundred and fifty dollars before and then another one hundred and fifty dollars after he survived the war. He was on a train to Elmira and then off to Riker's Island for training Benninsky did not see much combat because he got injured while working on a supply wagon. After Benninsky received a discharge, his injury worsened while doing manual labor. The labor agitated his injury, and he had difficulty making money. He thought poorly of Cleveland for reckoning his life and becoming his substitute after Benninsky died on August 18, 1887; Benninsky's final resting place was a regular gravesite in Steuben County. Though his death still made significant news across the nation.

On August 18, 1920, women gained the right to vote following Tennessee's ratification of the 19th Amendment with the necessary three-fourths vote.

On March 30, 1981, John Hinckley attempted to assassinate the 40th president, Ronald Reagan, outside Washington, DC. When Hinckley fired the first two shots, Alfred A. Antonucci, a sixty-eight-year-old gentleman from Garfield Heights in Cleveland, Ohio, wrestled Hinckley to the ground. Without Reagan realizing it, one bullet hit him in the chest, barely missing his heart. A Secret Service agent pushed him into a limousine and told the driver to head for the White House. Then, after realizing blood was coming out of the President's mouth, they immediately drove towards George Washington Hospital instead.

On March 30, 1870, the 15th Amendment to the United States Constitution was officially adopted, granting voting rights to Black men. The Secretary of State at the time, Hamilton Fish, proclaimed the 15th Amendment an official part of the US Constitution. On the day after March 31, Thomas Mundy Peterson became the first African American to participate in an election in New Jersey.

The ninth president, William Henry Harrison, elected in 1840, died of pneumonia in Washington, DC, on April 4, 1841.

The 16th president, Abraham Lincoln, elected in 1860, died on April 15, 1865, in Washington, DC, assassinated.

The twentieth president James Garfield, elected in 1880, died September 19, 1881, in Washington, DC, assassinated.

The twenty-fifth president William McKinley elected in 1900, died September 14, 1901, in Buffalo, New York, assassinated.

The twenty-ninth president Warren G. Harding, elected in 1920, died of a heart attack on August 2, 1923, in San Francisco, California.

The thirty-second president Franklin Delano Roosevelt elected in 1940, died on April 12, 1945, in Warm Springs, Georgia, due to bleeding to the brain.

The thirty-fifth President, John F. Kennedy, elected in 1960, died in Dallas, Texas, assassinated on November 22, 1963.

The fortieth President Ronald Reagan, elected in 1980, survived an assassination attempt on March 30, 1981, in Washington, DC

Thomas Hickey - John Hinckley

N-L: N 14th Letter. L 12th Letter. Alphabet

The second president to die on the zero factors was Abraham Lincoln. L —N Lincoln

The fourth president to die on the zero factor was McKinley. N - L McKinley

16th president: Abraham Lincoln — 17th President: Andrew Johnson — 18th President: Ulysses S. Grant

Ulysses S. Grant was the president when the United States turned 100 years old. Julia Dent, Grant's wife, died on December 14, 1902. George Washington died on December 14, 1799.

George Washington was the highest-ranked general of the Continental Army; his title was general and commander in chief of the Continental Army.

Ulysses S Grant eventually became the supreme union general during the Civil War.

James Monroe died July 4, 1831, 50 years before Ulysses S. Grant's grandson, Ulysses Simpson Grant, was born on July 4, 1881. James Monroe was shot and wounded at the Battle of Trenton after crossing the Delaware with George Washington.

25th President: William McKinley

When William McKinley was 18, He served in the Union as a private. His first taste of combat took place at the battle that helped create West Virginia become a new Union State at the battle of Carnifex Ferry. The battle took place on September 10, 1861. West Virginia Finally became a new State on June 20, 1863. Carnifex Ferry followed the first battle of the Civil War Philippi. William McKinley also saw combat at the Battle of Antietam, which became the Worst one-day battle in U.S. history. He fought through most of the war, and McKinley became highly respected among his peers. McKinley was

President during the Spanish-American war, making Puerto Rico a U.S. territory. He was also the last civil war veteran that served as President.

26th President: Theodore Roosevelt. 27th President: William Howard Taft. 28th President: Woodrow Wilson.

29th President: Warren G. Harding died on August 2, 1923. On August 2, 1776, most of the founding fathers signed the Declaration of Independence— 30th President, Calvin Coolidge, was the president when the country turned 150 years old. He was born July 4, 1872.

31st President Herbert Hoover — 32nd President Franklin Delano Roosevelt — 33th President Harry S Truman —

34th President Dwight Eisenhower, the supreme commander of the Allied Forces in World War II.

The 33rd president Harry S Truman died on December 26, 1972. Truman grew up in Independence, Missouri.- In World War I, he was a captain in field artillery and fought in France.

The 38th President Gerald Ford, a lieutenant commander in the Navy, died December 26, 2006 — 34 years apart from Harry S. Truman's death- Dwight Eisenhower was the 34th president.

35th President John F. Kennedy — 36th President Lyndon B Johnson — 37th President Richard Nixon—

38th Gerald Ford was the president when the country turned 200 years old.

38+38 equals 76 to 34 divided by 2: President Dwight Eisenhower.

Harry S. Truman and Gerald Ford died on Dec 26, with 12 and 26 being thirty-eight twice (or 76). Truman died in 1972, and Ford died in 2006, a difference of thirty-four. Dwight Eisenhower was the 34th United States president.

On December 26, 1776, George Washington crossed the Delaware with James Monroe, who was wounded and shot in his left shoulder at the Battle of Trenton.

Gerald Ford — Harry S Truman — Dwight Eisenhower

38+33+34 is 105 years 1776+105 = 1881 the 20th president

1776 plus 105=1881

voted July 2, 1776, Independence for/ Independence was declared July 4, 1776.

James Garfield was shot on July 2, 1881, eventually leading to his death. Two days later, Ulysses Simpson Grant was born on July 4, 1881. July 4, 1776, to July 4, 1881, is 105 years. Ulysses Simpson Grant was born on July 4, 1881. James Monroe died July 4, 1831, 50 years before Ulysses S. Grant's grandson's birth and 55 years after the Declaration of Independence. Ulysses S. Grant's only daughter, Nellie Grant, was born on July 4, 1855. James Monroe also died five years after the number three president Thomas Jefferson and the number two president, John Adams died. Totals five Thomas Jefferson and John Adams, the Author, and co-author of the Declaration of Independence. They both died 50 years after the Declaration of Independence. Before George Washington became the United States' first President; He stood as the President of the Constitutional Congress and the fourth President, James Madison, the Father of the Constitution, Equals five., The fifth president, James Monroe, was wounded at the Battle of Trenton after crossing the Delaware with George Washington.

16 Abraham Lincoln; 17 Andreu Johnson; 18 Ulysses S. Grant; 19 Rutherford B. Hayes; 20 James Garfield

The 20th president, James Garfield, was born on November 19, 1831.

James Garfield was born 32 years before the Gettysburg Address, in which Abraham Lincoln honored the soldiers who made the ultimate sacrifice to bring forth a "...new nation for life, liberty and the pursuit of happiness. That all men are created equal under God."

Charles Carol, the last surviving delegate of the 56 Signers of the Declaration of Independence, died on November 14, 1832. He was elected to Congress on July 4, 1776, which allowed him enough time to sign the Declaration of Independence. Charles Carol was born on September 19, 1737. James Garfield died September 19, 1881.

Charles Guiteau shot James Garfield at the Baltimore and Pontiac Railroad Station in Washington, DC.

After Charles Carol retired from Congress, he participated in the creation of the Baltimore and Ohio Railroad Company. Charles Carol died November 14, 1832, five days short of one year of the twentieth President James Garfield's birth on November 19, 1831. Charles Carol was the only Roman Catholic to sign the Declaration of Independence. Garfield was a preacher of the Disciples of Christ before he became the 20th president.

The founding fathers voted for Independence on July 2, 1776. Lyndon B. Johnson signed the Civil Rights Act on July 2, 1964. Martin Luther King, March 30, 1962 urged John F Kennedy to select Thurgood Marshall to fill a vacant seat in the Supreme Court. Thurgood Marshall became the first African-American Supreme Court justice. He was born July 2, 1908, 56 years before Lyndon B. Johnson signed the Civil Rights Act on July 2, 1964. There were 56 signers of the Declaration of Independence.

Thurgood Marshall was born July 2, 1908— 132 years after Independence from the founding fathers who voted for Independence on July 2, 1776. James Garfield was born on November 19, 1831 — 32 years before Abraham Lincoln honored the soldiers that made the ultimate sacrifice at the Gettysburg address on November 19, 1863. James Garfield was wounded and shot on July 2, 1881 — 105 years after Independence, which the Founding Fathers voted for on July 2, 1776.

Former Union general James Garfield, who was at the time a congressman from Ohio, addressed 5,000 people at the first commemoration Decoration day on May 30, 1868, for 20,000 Union and Confederate Soldiers buried at Arlington National Cemetery.

Robert E Lee was unsuccessful when he attempted to enter a northern state for the second time and Failed at The Battle of Gettysburg. Gen. George Meade led the Union Army, and it became the deadliest American Combat battle on American soil, with 23,000 Union casualties and 28,000 Confederate casualties. Gettysburg took place around the town of Gettysburg, Pennsylvania, on July 1-3, 1863, and it was 18 years from the day James Garfield was shot by Charles J. Guiteau on July 2, 1881.

James Garfield was born on November 19, 1831. In the Gettysburg Address on November 19, 1863, Abraham Lincoln honored the soldiers who sacrificed to bring forth a "...new nation for life, liberty and the pursuit of happiness. That all men are created equal under God." Thirty-two years apart from James Garfield's birth.

The last surviving signer of the Declaration of Independence, Charles Carroll, died November 14, 1832. the Vietnam War lasted from 1955 to 1975. The Battle of Ia Drang was fought November 14-18, 1965, and was the first significant engagement between the US Army and the People's Army of Vietnam.

James Garfield died Sept 19, 1881 / Charles Carol was born Sept 19, 1737

The turning point in the Revolutionary War began on September 19, 1777, at the first Battle of Saratoga at Freeman's Farm. The second Battle of Saratoga occurred on October 7, 1777, in Bemis Heights. The British surrendered on October 17, 1777. Many confusing events distinguished the British leadership and their disorganization that created the British downfall at the Battle of Saratoga, causing the turning point in the Revolutionary War in favor of the Americans.

The victory at Saratoga influenced King Louis XVI of France to believe that the Americans could stand tall against the British Army and then supported the Americans, resulting in the Treaty of Amity and Commerce and the Treaty of Alliance in Paris. This treaty created a military alliance against Great Britain. British General John Burgoyne became the original strategist in the Battle of Saratoga when Lord Germain, the British Secretary of State for the Colonies, allowed Burgoyne's plan. Burgoyne planned for a three-British force to conquer the Americans coming from three different directions at Saratoga and divide New England from the other American colonies.

Burgoyne wanted to lead a British force of over seven thousand men to come down from Canada. Then, Burgoyne`s troops would continue through the Lake Champlain Valley and capture Fort Ticonderoga. Burgoyne would then continue to travel south, seize Albany, New York, and join the second group of British soldiers under Colonel Barry St. Leger with two thousand soldiers. When Leger started his expedition to the Saratoga campaign on June 23, he and his men were instructed to advance towards the Oswego next to the Mohawk River Valley from Lake Ontario. Then, Leger would move into Albany with Burgoyne`s troops. The third force was supposed to have been overseen by William Howe, commander and chief of the British army who acted under the command of Germain, the British Secretary of State for the

Colonies, who approved Burgoyne`s plan that arranged for Howe's army to depart from New York City and move northward to the Hudson River Valley to gather with Burgoyne`s troops.

Burgoyne`s strategy became confusing, which was the beginning stage of the collapse of the British monarchy in the thirteen colonies. Before the Saratoga campaign began in June 1777, General William Howe sent a letter to Lord Germain in November 1776, requesting reinforcements to capture Albany and continue to Philadelphia. Then Howe changed his mind about Albany; instead, he thought the colonial capital of Philadelphia was more critical and informed Germain in a second letter. On February 28, 1777, Burgoyne presented his plan in writing to Lord Germain. Then, on May 18, 1777, Germain directed Howe to end the Philadelphia Campaign as soon as possible; in a letter, Germain wanted Howe to join the Saratoga campaign and take the commanding position. Unfortunately, the letter got to Howe after he left for Philadelphia. The Saratoga Campaign started on June 14, 1777. Then General Howe wrote a letter on July 17, which General Burgoyne received on August 3 at Fort Edward, informing Burgoyne that Howe would be leaving to sail with his army to capture Philadelphia and that General Sir Henry Clinton would oversee British forces in New York City.

On the Mohawk River, St. Leger`s Siege of Fort Stanwix lasted twenty days, beginning on August 2 and ending on August 22. The American Colonel Peter Gansevoort's men held Fort Stanwix and delayed St. Leger`s troops from advancing to Albany. Then Benedict Arnold, General in the Continental Army, came from Stillwater, New York, with a force of approximately eight hundred soldiers, deceived the British Colonel Barry St. Leger into believing false reports from a patriot posing as an informant for the British, Han-Yost Schuyler, who went into the Mohawks camp and convinced the Indians that Arnold had many more soldiers than St. Leger had. After St. Leger received this information from the Mohawks, The Indians evacuated Fort Stanwix because of combining data along with the Battle of Oriskany, which happened on August 6; St. Leger sent Sir John Johnson British forces with some Mohawk fighters to encounter a rebellious Militia. When General Nicholas Herkimer of the

Tryon County Militia discovered that the British had attacked the fort, He prepared around eight hundred men with the Oneida Indian scouts to fight. Then, after Johnson decided to ambush Herkimer`s Militia, The British troops began shooting. The Americans suffered many losses and withdrew to Fort Dayton. After the Indians suffered their casualties, it caused many doubts about their trust in the British.

Burgoyne, with two gigantic losses, St. Leger had withdrawn back to Lake Ontario on August 2. and worst of all, Howe had abandoned the New York campaign to fight in Philadelphia. Burgoyne also suffered heavy losses in his campaign previously to his specific troops. July 1 At the British capture of Fort Ticonderoga, General John Burgoyne forced the American General Arthur St. Clair to evacuate with the circumstances that British infantry directed by General Simon Fraser began to occupy the British soldiers up Sugar Loaf, now called the heights on Mount Defiance, which overlooks Fort Ticonderoga where they positioned their weaponry on the fort. St. Clair evacuated on July 6 without a fight.

Before Burgoyne arrived at Fort Edward, Burgoyne had to go through the swampy woodlands and challenging terrain. Burgoyne`s troops assembled forty bridges that Schuyler`s men destroyed. Schuyler`s men also destroyed dams, cut down trees, and blocked roads—Schuyler's strategy worked. The British, going slower than a turtle, ran exceptionally low on supplies. That is how Burgoyne arrived at Fort Edward. Burgoyne sent a German unit to Bennington, Vermont, to get hold of much-needed horses and supplies, but on August 16, The German unit was surrounded and overpowered by Gen. John Stark and Col. Seth Warner. Burgoyne lost close to a thousand men.

On August 10, Congress sent General Horatio Gates to be commander of the Northern Department. On August 19, Gates arrived at Albany to take command and replace General Philip Schuyler.

Burgoyne was close to Saratoga on the east bank of the Hudson River, and despite losing many men, he still wanted to try. Burgoyne ordered every camp from Skenesborogh to his location to evacuate their location and unite with the upcoming battle. Burgoyne had more men, but he lost his supply line.

General Henry Clinton wrote to Burgoyne on September 12, informing him that he would send men, but only after he completed his campaign to seize Fort Montgomery. The battle was not until October 6, which was the day before the second battle of Saratoga. Clinton wrote another letter to Burgoyne about the victory, but the Americans captured the messenger.

On September 19, the first Battle of Saratoga, at the Battle of Freeman's Farm, even though the British held their ground, they still lost more men than the Americans. The Americans had ninety killed and 240 wounded, and The British had 440 dead and close to seven hundred wounded.

October 7, The Second Battle of Saratoga at the Battle of Bemis Heights, Burgoyne was down to 5,000 men, and He estimated his supplies to last only for two more weeks. In comparison, Gates's army grew to 15,000 men. Burgoyne refused to retreat, which both Fraser and von Riedesel recommend. Gate sent a force command to Morgan to the front line. Arnold argued and suggested more troops were needed. Gates finally sent Colonel Enoch Poor's brigade to the battle. The battle began, and Arnold wanted to take command; Gates refused, but Arnold decided to take command anyway. Arnold rode out with a fresh brigade when he moved the British back.

Arnold`s leg was wounded during the battle. The British were overwhelmed. The Americans won the second Battle of Saratoga. Eventually, The Americans surrounded the British. The British surrendered on October 17, 1777.

The day after the Union Army defeated the Confederates at the Battle of Gettysburg marks The turning point of the Civil War at Vicksburg, Mississippi, in Warren County, May 18 - Jul 4, 1863. After the Union Siege that lasted 47 days, Lt. Gen. John C. Pemberton's Confederate Troops surrendered to Union General Ulysses S. Grant. Vicksburg was the last Central Confederate fortress. Having captured New Orleans and Memphis, 'the cities which the Mississippi River runs through' in early 1862, cutting off the States of Missouri, Arkansas, Louisiana, and Texas. Thus completing the Ananda plan originally presented by Winfield Scott, The Confederates lost their vital resources from the forty-seven-day siege at the Mississippi River, which made its way through the Confederate States. Then after The Battle of Port Hudson lasted from May 22 to July 9, 1863, Union troops took control of the entire Mississippi River.

September 19 and 20 - 1863, in Catoosa County and Walker County, Georgia. The Battle of Chickamauga was the second deadliest Civil War battle after the Battle of Gettysburg. Chickamauga was a Confederate offensive attack to recapture Chattanooga from the Union control of the railroad line that joined Chattanooga and Atlanta.

Confederate general Braxton Bragg knew he was outnumbered at Chattanooga after he discovered that Rosecrans's Union troops successfully crossed the Tennessee River around September 4. Braggs, unable to hold Chattanooga, retreated to Lafayette, Georgia, while the Union army entered Chattanooga on September 9. Bragg's counter-offensive plans included reinforcements guaranteed to reinforce and recapture Chattanooga. Braggs began to move his troops back to Chickamauga Creek on September 15. The battle started September 19, and the next day, more of Bragg's reinforcements overpowered Rosecrans's Union troops. Rosecrans realized retreat was the only choice. Rosecrans instructed his men to retreat to Chattanooga, where Braggs attacked the city by cutting off the Union's supply line. The Union army had 1,657 deaths. The Confederate 2,312 died. The twentieth President, James Garfield, died 18 years after the battle of Chickamauga, a struggle that Garfield fought. Chickamauga was the second deadliest battle in the Civil War. Major General Ulysses S. Grant arrived at Chattanooga and broke the Confederate siege. Then, the Battle of Chattanooga began, involving three individual battles over three days—the Battle of Orchard Knob under General George H. Thomas on November 23. In the Battle of Lookout Mountain under Union General Joseph Hooker on November 24 and the Battle of Missionary Ridge on November 25th, William T. Sherman received incorrect information, which led his Army of Tennessee away from Missionary Ridge and into Billy Goat Hill. There, Sherman's men attacked from the north at Tunnel Hill while Hooker's men struck Missionary Ridge from the south at Rossville Gap. General Thomas struck the center of Bragg's line, and as a result, the Union successfully drove the Confederates out of Chattanooga and into Georgia.

CHAPTER 21

Constantine the Great died May 22, 337 A.D. He became the first Christian Roman Emperor who legalized Christianity. Constantine's mother's name was Helena, and she was Greek. Legend says Constantine sent his mother in 324 for the true cross. She traveled to Jerusalem. She came to an area in which she uncovered three crosses. Some believe two crosses were the crosses on which the two thieves died, and the third was the cross on which Jesus died. To test, they instructed a leopard to touch each cross; when the leopard finally felt the third cross, the leper`s sickness healed. Constantine of Greece, 'the king during World War I,' was born on August 2, 1868. Napoleon of France was proclaimed consul for life On August 2, 1802. after Germany's President Paul Von Hindenburg died on August 2, 1934, it paved the way for Hitler to abolish the Office of President, and he officially became Fuhrer on August 19, 1934, from a referendum with 95 percent of the vote

On August 19, 1944, the liberation of Paris began precisely ten years after Hitler officially became the Fuhrer of Germany. Then after four years of being under the enemy control of the German Army, Paris was finally liberated on August 25, 1944. Twenty-three years before the liberation of France, The United States signed The Treaty of Berlin on August 25, 1921, because Congress refused to ratify the Treaty of Versailles. The Treaty of Versailles had been endorsed by Allied forces and signed by Germany on June 28, 1919, but many of the representatives in the United States Congress declined to accept the idea that a new coalition created inside the Treaty and titled the League of Nations would carry the power to decide whether The United States goes to war. Article 10 of the treaty would bring the United States into combat without any approval from Congress whatsoever. Woodrow Wilson wasn't entirely for the treaty. He had the Fourteen-Point Plan that he argued for when he was in the company of the "Big Four," which were the leaders of France, Great Britain, The United States, and Italy, at the Palace of Versailles in Paris, in which one of his points created the League of Nations. Woodrow Wilson wanted the League of Nations to police the World. France, England, Italy, and Japan took as the original participants, but the Senate dismissed any involvement from the United States. The United States signed a separate peace Treaty with Germany, The Treaty of Berlin, that declared the United States would enjoy all "rights, privileges, indemnities, reparations or advantages" conferred to it by the Treaty of Versailles but left out any mention of the League of Nations, which the United States never joined. The Treaty of Versailles was probably part of a recipe that created World War II since it made Germany pay very high repercussions from a written clause that blamed Germany for starting the war. The treaty made Germany lose much of their land, 10% in Europe, and all of its overseas colonies, including Saarland, a valuable area for its coal. The treaty also stated that Germany had to shrink their military, weakening the country. The other part of the ingredient that created World War II was the monster better known as the Furrier of Germany, Adolf Hitler.

The Treaty of Versailles was signed precisely five years after Archduke Franz.

A nationalist, Gavrilo Princip, assassinated Ferdinand and his wife Sophie on June 28, 1914, which ignited World War I.

The archduke went to Sarajevo in June 1914 to inspect the armed forces in Bosnia and Herzegovina, which Austria-Hungary annexed in October 1908. The Serbian nationalists titled The Black Hand thought the territories should have been part of Serbia, and the annexation had enraged A group of young

Serbian nationalists. A 19-year-old Gavrilo Princip was one of the nationalists to carry out the plan to assassinate the archduke. When his opportunity came, he shot Archduke Franz Ferdinand and his wife Sophie at open range while the couple traveled in their open-topped automobile, killing both more or less instantly. It was not long before the assassination that World War I exploded because a group of all countries combined, France, Britain, Ireland, and Russia, in a treaty, formed an alliance known as the Triple Entente. If any other country declared war against any government in the Triple Entente, Then by Treaty, the Triple Entente would stand together. The Central Powers were Germany and Austria-Hungry. Austria-Hungary became enraged and gave Serbia an ultimatum; one of the demands was to let Austria-Hungary perform its investigation into the assassination. Serbia agreed, but the momentum of preparing for war had the upper hand as pressure grew and communication between ally countries erupted on both sides. It became an unsuccessful, weak attempt to prevent conflict through negotiations. Then WW I became a reality after Austria-Hungary declared war on Serbia on July 28, 1914, exactly one month after assassinating Archduke Franz

Ferdinand and his wife, Sophie. On April 2, 1917, President Woodrow Wilson called for a Declaration of War against Germany. Congress approved the request, making it official that the United States was at war with Germany on April 6, 1917. On May 7, 1915, a German submarine sank a British passenger ship, the Lusitania, causing the deaths of almost 1,200 citizens, including 128 Americans. Germany voiced disappointment with the impartial government and pledged to amend the situation where the facts vindicated it. Germany said the Lusitania was one of the fastest and largest Government-funded vessels and that the English steamship company used the lives of citizens knowing that the vessel had ammunition on board. Then again, In March 1916, a German U-boat sank the Sussex, a French passenger ship. Dozens of people died, as well as several Americans. Afterward, the U.S. threatened to cut diplomatic relations with Germany. A reply from the Germans issued the Sussex pledged a promise to stop attacking merchant and passenger ships without proper warning. Nevertheless, on January 31, 1917, the Germans changed course, announcing they would pick up where they left off, making it unrestricted warfare for submarine combat, the Germans thought America was unprepared for battle, and it would help them win the war before America could even join the fighting on behalf of the Allies. In reaction to Germany's new announcement, The U.S. cut diplomatic relations with Germany on February 3. German submarines sank a series of U.S. merchant ships throughout February and March. Then, Germany sent a secret telegram to Mexico, which the British intelligence intercepted. The Zimmerman telegram offered an agreement between Germany and Mexico. Germany wanted to make a deal with Mexico. The Germans would help the Mexicans reclaim Texas, New Mexico, and Arizona. The land Mexico wrestled the United States for during the Mexican American War. In addition, Germany wanted Mexico to help influence Japan to switch sides in the conflict. Woodrow Wilson asked Congress for a declaration of war against Germany on April 2, 1917, and then Congress passed the bill on April 6, 1917. The United States declared war on April 7, 1917, 55 years after the Battle of Shiloh, April 6, 1862, through the next day, April 7, 1862. With a force of around 55,000, Albert Sidney Johnson commanded the Army of Mississippi at a central train station in Corinth, Mississippi. Corinth became a critical battleground location for the Union army. The Union needed the railroad, which would allow them to take control of the region. The victories of both Fort

Henry and Fort Donelson happened only two months before the Union planned to attack Corinth. The accomplishments of both Fort Henry and Fort Donelson also secured parts of Tennessee. The six divisions that made up Grant's army of Tennessee consisted of roughly 45,000 men— Grant's superior Union, Maj. Gen. Henry W. Halleck ordered Grant to wait for the arrival of Maj—Gen—Don Carlos Buell's Army of Ohio with around 20,000 men. Grant's army remained at Pittsburg Landing, Tennessee, on the river's west bank at a small Shiloh Church.

The Confederate General Albert Johnston set out from Corinth with around 40,000 men on April 3rd. His main objective was to catch Grant's army off guard before Buell's army arrived at Grant's location. Johnston wanted to begin the attack on April 4th, but heavy rains delayed his army. The heavy rain held up Buell's army as well. April 6, 1862, early in the morning, about three hours before the break of dawn, Col. Everett Peabody sent a patrol of 250 Union Soldiers to check to see if the Confederate position might be in the vicinity and discovered by the decision made by Col. Everett Peabody even though he was in defiance of his order because the Union did not want any distraction that could start the battle before the reinforcements arrived. Peabody's soldiers located and warned the Union Army and avoided an all-out surprise attack on Grant's Union Army.

Peabody's warning, however, did not stop an unyielding attack by the Confederate Army that started around 9 am at an area nicknamed Hornet's Nest.

Prentiss led a Union division at the Hornet's Nest with 5,400 Union men to hold off the Confederate Army, but after seven hours of fighting, 5,400 men shrank to 500 men. William Hervey Larmme Wallace led another Union Division that entered the Hornet's Nest to aid Prentiss's division, but The Union seemed so unprepared when The Confederate Army surrounded both divisions. Wallace then decided to call for his division to escape, and, He turned out to be mortally wounded when he tried to escape himself.

During the confrontation at Hornet's Nest, Confederate commanding General Albert Sidney Johnston was wounded and shot in his right leg. He did not think the wound was life-threatening, but He lost too much blood and died because of a torn artery.

Albert S. Johnston was the highest-ranked officer in the Civil War to die while serving in combat. General P.G. T. Beauregard took control of the Confederate forces in the Battle of Shiloh after Albert S. Johnston`s death.

The Confederates failed a final offensive assault to break the Union Army. Beauregard called off the assault at nightfall.

April 7, 1862, The reinforced Union Army numbered around 45,000 men, with Don Carlos Buell's Army arriving on April 6, 1862. Now with the upper hand, the Union outnumbered the Confederates, that had their casualties, including their Commanding Officer, Albert S. Johnston, who died in battle. The Confederates now had less than 30,000 men. The Union sprang a solid counter-attack at daybreak, and the Union forces were able to recapture the Hornet's Nest.

After intense fighting in the early afternoon, Beauregard threw in a sequence of effective counterpunches around the Shiloh Church, which drove Union forces back slightly. But ultimately, reality caught up to Beauregard, and he decided that he had been outgunned and ordered a retreat. Grant's superior, Union Maj. Gen. Henry W. Halleck, made it to Pittsburg Landing to take command in the field. It wasn't until late May that Halleck led the Union Army and captured the Town of Corinth. Newspapers and Public Opinion blamed Grant for the massive loss at Shiloh, but Lincoln's responded, "I can't spear this man he fights." Union had 13,047 casualties in the Battle of Shiloh, 1,754 Union were killed, 8,408 Union were wounded, and 2,885 Union Soldiers were missing. The Confederates had 10,699 casualties. There were 1,728 Confederates killed and 8,012 wounded. The Battle of Shiloh had 23,746 casualties and was the bloodiest battle in American history up to that time.

At 5:45 a.m. on Nov. 11, 1918, Allied forces and Germany signed an armistice that went into effect at 11 a.m. on the "11th hour of the 11th day of the 11th month. A year later Wilson's proclamation said, "...reflections of Armistice Day will be filled with solemn pride in the heroism of those who died in the country's service and with gratitude for the victory, both because of the thing from which it has freed us and because of the opportunity it has given America to show her sympathy with peace and justice in the councils of the nations".

France observes Nov. 11 as Armistice Day. Canada recognizes the date as "Remembrance Day," and Great Britain acknowledges the second Sunday of each November. In 1954, Dwight Eisenhower signed a bill that the holiday's name be changed to Veterans Day to recognize all US Veterans from every war and conflict.

Washington State`s named after George Washington. On November 11, 1889, Washington became the 42nd State when the 23rd President, Benjamin Harrison, presided in the White House. Benjamin Harrison fought in the Civil

War in the same way as his Grandfather, the 9th President William Henry Harrison, fought in the War of 1812.

In 1868, Constantine I of Greece's mother`s name was Olga. She was from Russia and died on June 18, 1926—one hundred eleven years after The battle of Waterloo on June 18th, 1815. Waterloo was the battle in which Napoleon was captured and exiled to the Island of Helena. Helena was Constantine, the Great Mother's name.

From Napoleon in 1802- 66 years to the birth of Constantine I of Greece in 1868 'king of Greece during World War I' -66 years to Hitler in 1934—to Napoleon died on St. Helena. There are 66 books in the Protestant Bible.

EPILOGUE

George Washington was the United States' first president; his inauguration date was April 30, 1789. George Washington's Stepchildren, John Parke Custis, and Martha Park Custis were the children of Martha Washington. Martha Park Custis died as a teenager while she had an epileptic seizure. Then John Park Custis died November 5, 1781, while serving as an aid to Washington during the Siege of Yorktown in 1781. The probable cause of death was Typhus. After John Park Custis died at age 26, The Washingtons raised his two youngest children, John Parke Custis and Martha Park Custis, at Mount Vernon. George Washington Custis was born on April 30, 1781, and died on October 10, 1857, at 76 years old. George Washington's first inauguration was on April 30, 1789. George Washington Adams, the first son of John Quincy Adams, died on April 30, 1829. George Washington`s stepson, John Park Custis, passed away the same day as John Hanson, who won the November 5, 1781 election and became the first President of Congress of the Confederation. some suggest that John Hanson became the United States' first President under the Articles of Confederation.

The Continental Congress adopted the Articles of Confederation on November 15, 1777, but not signed by all thirteen States until March 1, 1781. The Articles of Confederation gave too much power to the states. The Constitution then replaced the Articles of Confederation on March 4, 1789, and created a stronger central government with three branches of government along with the Bill of Rights. The Constitution gave control to the Central Government to tax the citizens of the United States. George Washington Custis had four children, including Mary Ann Custis, who became the wife of Robert E Lee, the Confederate general during the Civil War. Mary Anna Custis Lee died November 5, 1873, 92 years after her grandfather death. John Park Custis died November 5, 1781. Exactly one year before Mary Anna Custis died, Ulysses S. Grant was reelected to his second term as the eighteenth president of The United States on November 5, 1872. As Commanding Union General in the Civil War, Ulysses S. Grant accepted Robert E Lee's surrender on April 9, 1865, at Appomattox Courthouse.

The first President George Washington's wife's family line became directly connected to the Confederacy when Mary Anna Custis married Robert E Lee. After the 10th President, John Tyler, served his term as president of the United States, He later became elected to the Confederate House of Representatives. however, before he could take a chair, he died on January 18, 1862, in Richmond, Virginia, the Capital of the Confederacy. The second President, John Adams, wrote to his wife on July 3, 1776. He thought July 2, 1776, would be the most memorable date in history." The Second Day of July 1776 will be the most memorable epoch in the history of America. Apt to believe that it will be celebrated by succeeding generations as a significant anniversary Festival. It ought to be commemorated as the Day of Deliverance by solemn Acts of Devotion to God Almighty. It ought to be solemnized with Pomp and Parade, with Shews, Games, Sports, Guns, Bells, Bonfires, and Illuminations from one End of this Continent to the other from this Time forward forever more". The 20th President, James Garfield, suffered being shot and wounded on July 2, 1881, 105 years after July 2, 1776. The third President, Thomas Jefferson, was the Author of the Declaration of Independence on July 4, 1776, and died exactly 50 years after July 4, 1826.

The 30th president Calvin Coolidge was the president when the United States became a hundred and fifty years old on July 4, 1926. He was born July

4. 1872. Thomas Jefferson was born on April 13, 1743. Calvin Coolidge's son Calvin Coolidge Junior was born on April 13, 1908, 165 years after Thomas Jefferson's birth. April 13, 1865, Lincoln's last full day before John Wilkes Booth shot him the next day.

The fourth president James Madison, the father of the Constitution and the last surviving founding father of the United States to die. There were thirty-nine signers to the Constitution The 40th president Ronald Reagan was the first not to die in office after being elected on a zero year, ever since William Henry Harrison, who was also elected on a zero year, died and became the first president to die in office. Of all the presidents that were in office, Regan was the thirty-ninth

The fifth president James Monroe died July 4, 1831, 55 years after the Declaration of Independence. James Monroe also died five years after the passing of Thomas Jefferson and John Adams on July 4, 1926.

James Monroe also died 50 years before the grandson of Ulysses S. Grant, Ulysses Simpson Grant birth on July 4, 1881.

Zachary Taylor's daughter Sarah Knox Taylor died on September 15, 1835. Her husband was Jefferson Davis at the time of her death. Twenty-six years later Jefferson Davis became the president of the Confederacy during the Civil War.

Zachary Taylor became a war hero when he fought in the Mexican-American war. He then ran for president and became the twelfth president of the United States. Even though Zachary Taylor lived as a slaveholder, he stood against the spread of slavery to the new US territories that expanded the United States after the American-Mexican War ended. Zachary Taylor had a younger brother Joseph Pannell Taylor a Brig—Gen. in the Union Army. Zachary Taylor's son Richard Taylor fought for the Confederacy as a lieutenant general. Richard Taylor died on April 12, 1879, exactly 18 years after the Civil War began on April 12, 1861. His father, Zachary Taylor, died July 9, 1850, 18 years before the 14th Amendment came on July 9, 1868. be ratified.

Sarah Knox Taylor died September 15, 1835, exactly 22 years before the 27th President William Howard Taft's birth on September 15, 1857. Former president William Howard Taft dedicated the Lincoln Memorial on May 30, 1922. At that time, William Howard Taft stood as the Supreme Court Justice when he committed the monument. When William Howard Taft preceded as President, He signed a bill on February 11, 1911, to design the memorial.

50 years before William Howard Taft signed the bill on February 11, 1911
Abraham Lincoln's Farewell Address February 11, 1861

*My Friends—No one, not in my situation, can appreciate
my feeling of sadness at this parting. To this place, and the kindness
of these people, I owe everything. Here I have lived a quarter of a century
and have passed from a young to an old man. Here my children
have been born, and one is buried. I now leave, not knowing when, or
whether ever, I may return, with a task before me greater than that
which rested upon Washington. Without the assistance of that
Divine Being, who ever attended him, I cannot succeed.
With that assistance I cannot fail. Trusting in Him, who can go with me,
and remain with you and be everywhere for good,
let us confidently hope that all will yet be well.
To His care commending you, as I hope in your prayers
you will commend me, I bid you an affectionate farewell.*

-Abraham Lincoln

BOOK SOURCES

Graff, Henry F. 1996. *The Presidents: A Reference History*. New York: Simon and Schuster MacMillian.

Greenman, Barbara. 2009. *US Presidents and First Ladies*. San Diego: Thunder Bay Press.

Library of Congress. 2020. *Chronological List Presidents, First Ladies, and Vice Presidents of the United States*. Washington DC, February 20.

Merry, Robert W. 2017. President McKinley: Architect of the American Century. New York: Simon and Schuster.

The Poynter Institute. 2009. The Kennedy's: America's Front Page Family. Kansas City: Andrew McMeel Publishing.

ELECTRONIC SOURCES

Grammarly contributed to this text by responding to these AI prompts:

Prompts created by Grammarly
- "Make it more detailed"
- "Make it informative"
- "Clean up notes"
- "Shorten it"
- "Make it more descriptive"
- "Make it direct"
- "Make it inspirational"
- "Make it engaging"
- "Improve it"
- "Make it persuasive"
- "Make it assertive"

"10 Facts: Battles for Chattanooga." American Battlefield Trust, November 22, 2021. https://www.battlefields.org/learn/articles/10-facts-battles-chattanooga.

"14th Amendment to the U.S. Constitution: Civil Rights (1868)." National Archives and Records Administration. National Archives and Records Administration, September 8, 2020. https://www.archives.gov/milestone-documents/14th-amendment.

"1872 United States Presidential Election Ulysses S Grant Was Reelected President November 5, 1872 ." Wikipedia. Wikimedia Foundation, June 29, 2022. https://en.wikipedia.org/wiki/1872_United_States_presidential_election.

"1934: Hitler Declared Führer after Referendum." History.info. Motus d.o.o., August 1, 2019. https://history.info/on-this-day/1934-hitler-declaredfuhrer-after-referendum/.

"56 Signers of the Declaration of Independence- Memorial (U.S. National Park Service)." National Parks Service. U.S. Department of the Interior, October 24, 2020. https://www.nps.gov/places/000/56-signers-of-the-declaration-of-independence-memorial.htm.

"86 Union Soldiers along with Commander Robert Anderson Surrendered." Accessed May 31, 2022. https://findanyanswer.com/who-won-thebattle-at-fort-sumter.

"Aaron Burr Senior's Birthday, January 4, 1716." geni_family_tree, April 27, 2022. https://www.geni.com/people/Rev-AaronBurr/6000000001362917056.

"Abigail Adams Birth." WHHA (en-US). The White House Historical Association, January 16, 2019. https://www.whitehousehistory.org/bios/abigailadams.

"Abigail Adams November 22, 1744." Wikipedia. Wikimedia Foundation, June 13, 2022. https://en.wikipedia.org/wiki/Abigail_Adams.

"Abigail Louisa Louise (Adams) Johnson." WikiTree. INTERESTING.COM, INC, November 27, 2020. https://www.wikitree.com/wiki/Adams-10211.

"Abraham Baldwin." Wikipedia. Wikimedia Foundation, June 10, 2022. https://en.wikipedia.org/wiki/Abraham_Baldwin.

"Abraham Lincoln and His Son Tad, Who on This Day Just Turned 12 Years Old, Visited Richmond, Virginia, April 4, 1865. ." Abraham Lincoln entering Richmond Virginia. Son of the South. Accessed June 11, 2022. http://sonofthesouth.net/slavery/abraham-lincoln/abraham-lincoln-richmond.htm.

"Abraham Lincoln II." Military Wiki. Accessed June 5, 2022. https://military-history.fandom.com/wiki/Abraham_Lincoln_II.

Admin. "March 4, 1776, George Washington Took Dorchester Heights," American History, March 4, 2016. http://blog.alssar.org/uncategorized/george-washington-takes-dorchesterheights/.

Admin. "Jefferson Davis Elected Provisional President of the Confederate The States of America 160 Years Ago #OnThisDay #OTD (Feb 9, 1861)." RetroNewser, February 10, 2021. https://retronewser.com/2021/02/09/jeffersondavis-elected-provisional-president-of-the-confederate-states-of-america/.

Admin. "June 6, 2015 – Robert F. Kennedy Assassinated June 6, 1968." Troy Historic Village - Where history lives, April 10, 2017. https://www.troyhistoricvillage.org/june-6-2015-robert-f-kennedy-assassinated-june-6-1968/.

"After Fighting for the Abolition of Slavery for 25 Years, William Lloyd Garrison Believed the Republic Had Been Corrupted from the Start." PBS. Public Broadcasting Service. Accessed June 19, 2022. https://www.pbs.org/wgbh/americanexperience/features/the-abolitionistsgarrison-burns-constitution/.

"Agustin De Iturbide the First Emperor of Mexico Was Born in Valladolid, on Sept 27, 1783." Encyclopedia.com. Encyclopedia.com, June 2, 2022. https://www.encyclopedia.com/people/history/mexican-history-biographies/agustin-de-iturbide.

"Alexander Hamilton Wrote Two-Thirds of the Federalist Papers." Constitution of the United States. US Constitution, April 25, 2022.

https://constitutionus.com/presidents/important-roles/was-hamilton-a-federalist/.

"America Signed a Peace Treaty with Germany August 25, 1921." US Peace Treaty with Germany - World War I Document Archive. World War I Document Archive, May 20, 2009. https://wwi.lib.byu.edu/index.php/US_Peace_Treaty_with_Germany.

Americanwarsus. "Battle of Princeton - January 3, 1777, in Princeton, New Jersey." American Revolutionary War. American Revolutionary War, October 17, 2018. https://revolutionarywar.us/year-1777/battle-of-princeton/.

Andrew Glaws. "Star-spangled banner" becomes U.S. National Anthem, March 3, 1931 ..., March 3, 2018. https://www.politico.com/story/2018/03/03/star-spangled-banner-becomes-us-national-anthem-march-3-1931-432140.

"Andrew Jackson January 30 ATTEMPTED ASSINATION." Biography.com. A&E Networks Television, November 16, 2021. https://www.biography.com/us-president/andrew-jackson.

"Andrew Jackson." Wikipedia. Wikimedia Foundation, June 10, 2022. https://en.wikipedia.org/wiki/Andrew_Jackson.

Anirudh, Happy, Learnodo Newtonic, Izaiha, and Leon Jr Connell. "Battle of Shiloh ." Learnodo Newtonic, September 12, 2018. https://learnodo-newtonic.com/battle-of-shiloh-facts.

Anirudh, Jc, Davis, Orion, Learnodo Newtonic, Vivian, and Joshua Pfaff. "Jefferson Davis's Father, Samuel Davis, Named His Son after Thomas Jefferson." Learnodo Newtonic, September 14, 2018. https://learnodo-newtonic.com/jefferson-davis-facts.

"Ann Phoebe Penn Dagworthy Charlton B. 6 February 1756 d. 8 July 1830." Ann Phoebe Penn Dagworthy Charlton b. 6 February 1756 d. 8 July 1830 - Rodovid EN, November 2, 2006. https://en.rodovid.org/wk/Person:44070.

"Arranged for the Withdrawal of Remaining Spanish Forces." Encyclopedia.com. Encyclopedia.com, June 2, 2022. https://www.encyclopedia.com/humanities/encyclopedias-almanacs-transcripts-and-maps/cordoba-treaty-1821.

"Article, Opponents Argued, Ceded the War Powers of the U.S. Government to the League's Council." Why was the Treaty of Versailles signed after World War I a failure - DailyHistory.org. DailyHistory.org, July 20, 2021. https://dailyhistory.org/Why_was_the_Treaty_of_Versailles_signed_after_World_War _I_a_failure.

"Aug 28, 1963, CE: Martin Luther King Jr. Gives 'I Have a Dream' Speech." National Geographic Society. National Geographic Society, October 18, 2021. https://www.nationalgeographic.org/thisday/aug28/i-havedream-speech/.

"August 6, 1965, AN Act Which Was Signed into Law." Constitutional Rights Foundation. Constitutional Rights Foundation. Accessed August 3, 2022. https://www.crf-usa.org/bill-of-rights-in-action/bria-12-2-b-race-andvoting-in-the-segregated-south.

"Austria-Hungary Declares War on Serbia." History.com. A&E Television Networks, July 27, 2020. https://www.history.com/this-day-in-history/austria-hungary-declares-war-on-serbia.

Avery, Kevin, trans. "Mehetabel Wellington Sherman (1688-1776) - Find a..." Find a Grave, November 2, 2005. https://www.findagrave.com/memorial/12241819/mehetabel-sherman.

Axelrod of WAYRUN, Jason. "The Gettysburg Address - November 19, 1863, | Abraham Lincoln." Civil War Talk. CIVILWARTALK, LLC, November 19, 2016. https://civilwartalk.com/threads/the-gettysburg-addressnovember-19-1863.128924/.

Balestrieri, Steve. "Joseph E. Johnson Died of Pneumonia." SOFREP, August 6, 2020. https://sofrep.com/news/april-26-1865-gen-joseph-johns-tonsurrenders-the-army-of-tennessee/.

Bannister, Craig. "Three Presidents Have Died on the Fourth of July – Two on the Same Day." CNSNews.com. Media Resource Center, July 3, 2018. https://www.cnsnews.com/blog/craig-bannister/three-presidents-have-diedfourth-july-two-same-day.

Barela, Nova. "The 26th President Theodore Roosevelt: 'Speak Softly and

Carry a Big Stick, You Will Go Far.'" Reference. IAC Publishing, June 1, 2022. https://www.reference.com/history/theodore-roosevelt-the-life-andlegacy-president.

"Battle of Baltimore a Sea/Land Battle Fought between the British Invaders and Americans." Wikipedia. Wikimedia Foundation, June 1, 2022. https://en.wikipedia.org/wiki/Battle_of_Baltimore.

"Battle of Baltimore." Wikipedia. Wikimedia Foundation, June 1, 2022. https://en.wikipedia.org/wiki/Battle_of_Baltimore.

"Battle of Belmont." Wikipedia. Wikimedia Foundation, February 14, 2022. https://en.wikipedia.org/wiki/Battle_of_Belmont.

"Battle of Chickamauga (Sep. 19–20, 1863) Summary & Facts." Totally History. Totallyhistory.com, January 9, 2014. https://totallyhistory.com/battleof-chickamauga/.

"Battle of Lookout Mountain." Military Wiki, November 24, 1863. https://military-history.fandom.com/wiki/Battle_of_Lookout_Mountain.

"Battle of Pensacola (1814)." Battle of Pensacola (1814) - Pensapedia, the Pensacola encyclopedia, January 25, 2017. https://www.pensapedia.com/wiki/Battle_of_Pensacola_(1814).

"Battle of Philippi (1861)." Wikipedia. Wikimedia Foundation, January 6, 2022. https://en.wikipedia.org/wiki/Battle_of_Philippi_(1861).

"Battle Of Trenton Artillery Capt." Wikipedia. Wikimedia Foundation, October 6, 2021. https://en.wikipedia.org/wiki/Order_of_battle_of_the_Battle_of_Trenton.

Beckenbaugh, Terry. "Civil War on the Western Border: The Missouri-Kansas Conflict, 1854-1865." Battle of Island Mound | Civil War on the Western Border: The Missouri-Kansas Conflict, 1854-1865. Accessed December 5, 2023. https://civilwaronthewesternborder.org/encyclopedia/battle-island-mound.

Bell, Alyssa, Samantha Han, Zach Thomas, and Alyssa Crawford. "Helen Keller Theodore Roosevelt and 500,000 Signatures." National Woman's Party Project. Accessed July 27, 2022.

https://depts.washington.edu/moves/NWP_project_ch1.shtml.

"Benjamin Harrison V." The Society of the Descendants of the Signers of the Declaration of Independence. Accessed June 26, 2022. https://www.dsdi1776.com/benjamin-harrison-v/.

"Benjamin Harrison V: Fifth Governor of Virginia." Revolutionary War. Revolutionary War, March 4, 2020. https://www.revolutionary-war.net/benjamin-harrison-v/.

Biography.com Editors. "Andrew Jackson Joined a Militia." Biography.com. A&E Networks Television, November 16, 2021. https://www.biography.com/us-president/andrew-jackson.

Biography.com Editors. "Robert Todd Lincoln." Biography.com. A&E Networks Television, July 21, 2020. https://www.biography.com/political-figure/robert-todd-lincoln.

BlackPast, contributed by: "(1857) Abraham Lincoln, 'the Dred Scott Decision and Slavery' •." (1857) Abraham Lincoln, "The Dred Scott Decision and Slavery" •, October 5, 2019. https://www.blackpast.org/african-american-history/1857-abraham-lincoln-dred-scott-decision-and-slavery/.

"Bladensburg." American Battlefield Trust. American Battlefield Trust. Accessed June 2, 2022. https://www.battlefields.org/learn/war-1812/battles/bladensburg.

"Britain Abolishes the Slave Trade March 25, 1807." OnThisDay.com. This Day Pte. Ltd., May 12, 1789. https://www.onthisday.com/photos/britainabolishes-the-slave-trade.

Britannica, T. Editors of Encyclopaedia. "John Wilkes Booth Was Born, May 10, 1838." Encyclopædia Britannica. Encyclopædia Britannica, inc., May 6, 2022. https://www.britannica.com/biography/JohnWilkes-Booth.

Britannica, T. Editors of Encyclopaedia. ed. "Daniel D. Tompkins." Encyclopædia Britannica. Encyclopædia Britannica, inc., June 17, 2022. https://www.britannica.com/biography/Daniel-D-Tompkins.

Britannica, T. Editors of Encyclopaedia. "Nathan Hale." Encyclopædia Britannica. Encyclopædia Britannica, inc., June 2, 2022. https://www.bri-

tannica.com/biography/Nathan-Hale.
Britannica, T. Editors of Encyclopaedia. "Anton J. Cermak Mayor Died March 6, 1933." Encyclopædia Britannica. Encyclopædia Britannica, inc., May 5, 2022. https://www.britannica.com/biography/Anton-J-Cermak.
Britannica, T. Editors of Encyclopaedia. "Benjamin Lincoln Died May 9, 1810." Encyclopædia Britannica. Encyclopædia Britannica, inc., May 5, 2022. https://www.britannica.com/biography/Benjamin-Lincoln.
Britannica, T. Editors of Encyclopaedia. "Confiscation Acts." Encyclopædia Britannica. Encyclopædia Britannica, inc. Accessed July 16, 2022. https://www.britannica.com/event/Confiscation-Acts.
Britannica, T. Editors of Encyclopaedia. "Constantine I of Greece Was Born August 2, 1868." Encyclopædia Britannica. Encyclopædia Britannica, inc. Accessed June 30, 2022. https://www.britannica.com/biography/Constantine-I-king-of-Greece.
Britannica, T. Editors of Encyclopaedia. "United States Presidential Election of 1944." Encyclopædia Britannica. Encyclopædia Britannica, inc. Accessed June 25, 2022. https://www.britannica.com/event/United-States-presidential-election-of1944.
Britannica, T. Editors of Encyclopaedia. "Zachary Taylor." Encyclopædia Britannica. Encyclopædia Britannica, inc. Accessed June 5, 2022. https://www.britannica.com/biography/Zachary-Taylor.
Britton, Rick. "James Monroe: Injured at the Battle of Trenton." Journal of the American Revolution, August 28, 2016. https://allthingsliberty.com/2013/01/james-monroe-bona-fide-hero-of-theamerican-revolution/.
Bruce, K.S. "Ted Jr.'s Own Son, Quentin, Was Also in the First D-Day Wave, Landing on Omaha Beach." InsideHook, June 6, 2019. https://www.insidehook.com/article/history/teddy-roosevelt-jr-tough-estold-man-wwii.
Bubis, Dan & Jax. "North Carolina Is the First State to Call for Independence - April 12, 1776." April 12, 1776, voted for independence in North

Carolina. Revolutionary-War-and-Beyond.com, April 12, 2013. https://www.revolutionary-war-and-beyond.com/north-carolina-first-statecall-for-independence.html.

"Bull Run McDowell's Troops Were Stopped at Bull Run by Brig. Gen." American Battlefield Trust. American Battlefield Trust, May 2022. https://www.battlefields.org/learn/civil-war/battles/bull-run.

Buntinaldo, Benwardo, and A WordPress Commenter. "Just 18 Words." Just Brazil, May 26, 2022. http://www.justbrazil.org/when-did-slavery-end-in-brazil/.

Burr, Sherri. "Princeton & Slavery | and John Pierre Burr Birthday/and Deathday." Princeton University. The Trustees of Princeton University. Accessed June 2, 2022. https://slavery.princeton.edu/stories/john-pierre-burr.

C., Manon. "History Fact: It Happened on August 19, the Liberation of Paris." Sortiraparis.com, August 19, 2021. https://www.sortiraparis.com/arts-culture/histoirepatrimoine/articles/257934-history-fact-it-happened-on-august-19-the-liberation-of-paris/lang/en.

Calder, Anna. The German Government will treat the cases of the American steamers Cushing and Gulflightaccording to the same principles. The Lusitania Resource, March 26, 2011. https://www.rmslusitania.info/primarydocs/german-response/.

"Calvin Coolidge Accepts the Republican Nomination for President, Aug. 14, 1924." NYPL Digital Collections. The New York Public Library. Accessed June 5, 2022. https://digitalcollections.nypl.org/items/510d47d9b11c-a3d9-e040-e00a18064a99.

Cano, Ruddy. "Rank of General of the Armies Was Only Given Twice in US History." We Are The Mighty. We Are The Mighty, July 5, 2021. https://www.wearethemighty.com/popular/only-2-six-star-generals/.

Carlton, Genevieve. "The Shocking Story of the Woman Who Tried to Assassinate Gerald Ford - and Missed by Just Six Inches." All That's Interesting. All That's Interesting, May 16, 2022. https://allthatsinteresting.com/sara-jane-moore.

Carter, Chris. "20 August 1866: The American Civil War Officially Ends." MoneyWeek, August 20, 2020. https://moneyweek.com/405018/20-august-1866-the-american-civil-war-officially-ends.

"Chapter 3: Crozer Seminary." The Martin Luther King, Jr., Research and Education September 14, 1948. Stanford University, February 23, 2022. https://kinginstitute.stanford.edu/king-papers/publications/autobiographymartin-luther-king-jr-contents/chapter-3-crozer-seminary.

"Charles Adams Born May 29, 1770." Wikipedia. Wikimedia Foundation, December 19, 2021. https://en.wikipedia.org/wiki/Charles_Adams_(1770%E2%80%931800).

"Charles Adams (1770–1800)." Wikipedia. Wikimedia Foundation, December 19, 2021. https://en.wikipedia.org/wiki/Charles_Adams_(1770%E2%80%931800).

"Charles Carroll Elected July 4, 1776, and Most Information about Charles Carroll." Wikipedia. Wikimedia Foundation, June 25, 2022. https://en.wikipedia.org/wiki/Charles_Carroll_of_Carrollton.

"Chattanooga Union Forces Had Driven Confederate Troops Away from Chattanooga, Tennessee, into Georgia." American Battlefield Trust. American Battlefield Trust, May 2022. https://www.battlefields.org/learn/civilwar/battles/chattanooga.

Cheshire, Marc. "Resolved, Unanimously, July 9, 1776." CROTON, July 2, 2019. https://crotonhistory.org/2013/07/05/resolved-unanimously-july-91776/.

Chestnut, Trichita. "There Is No East, No West…:' Dr. Martin Luther King, Jr. Visits Cold ..." Accessed June 28, 2022. https://www.archives.gov/files/research/foreign-policy/cold-war/berlin-wall1962-1987/dvd/pdfs/vingettes/7_V-4.pdf.

Clayborne, Carson, and Lewis, D. L. "Martin Luther King, Jr." Encyclopædia Britannica. Encyclopædia Britannica, inc. Accessed June 2, 2022. https://www.britannica.com/biography/Martin-Luther-King-Jr.

Clot, Nathalie, trans. "Napoleon of France Was Proclaimed Consul for Life August 2, 1802." napoleon.org. Fondation Napoléon. Accessed June 30, 2022. https://www.napoleon.org/en/history-of-the-two-empires/timelines/fromlife-consulship-to-the-hereditary-empire-1802-1804/.

"Col Peyton H. Colquitt - Civil War Officer. during the Civil War, He Became the Commander of Gist's Brigade. on September ...: Chickamauga, Famous Graves, Cemeteries." Pinterest, September 22, 2016. https://www.pinterest.com/pin/col-peyton-h-colquitt-civil-war-officer-during-the-civil-war-he-became-the-commander-of-gists-brigade-on-september—499195939930035295/.

"College of New Jerseybecame| Princeton University in 1896." Princeton University. The Trustees of Princeton University. Accessed August 3, 2022. https://library.princeton.edu/special-collections/topics/college-new-jersey.

Congress, Author: United States. "Allows Slaveowners to Seize and Arrest Fugitive Slaves and Present Written or Oral Proof to an Official to Reclaim Their Property." (1793)." Encyclopedia Virginia. Virginia Humanities, February 12, 1793. https://encyclopediavirginia.org/entries/an-act-respecting-fugitives-from-justice-and-persons-escaping-from-the-service-of-t heir-masters-1793/.

Conradt, Stacy. "4th Of July at a Fund-Raising Event." Mental Floss. Mental Floss, November 21, 2014. https://www.mentalfloss.com/article/60224/grave-sightings-zachary-taylor.

"Day of Infamy: FDR's Response on December 7, 1941 - Google Arts & Culture." Google. Google. Accessed June 6, 2022. https://artsandculture.google.com/exhibit/day-of-infamy-fdr-s-response-ondecember-7-1941-u-s-national-archives/QRXZUqsM?hl=en.

"December 14, Congressman James Ashley, Republican of Ohio, Introduced a Bill in Support of a Constitutional Amendment to Ban Slavery." 13th Amendment site. HarpWeek, LLC. Accessed June 27, 2022. https://13thamendment.harpweek.com/HubPages/CommentaryPage.asp?Commentary=01Timeline1863.

"December 21, 1945 - General Patton Dies Following Mysterious Car Accident." This Day in Automotive History. A Cars & Copy Production, December 21, 2021. https://automotivehistory.org/general-patton-dies-following-caraccident/.

Denial, Catherine. "Bleeding Kansas 55 People Died." Teachinghistory.org. National Education Clearinghouse. Accessed May 30, 2022. https://teachinghistory.org/history-content/ask-a-historian/25650.

Dobson, Rachel. "Col. Peyton H. Colquitt Birth/Death." Find a Grave. Find a Grave. Accessed June 1, 2022. https://es.findagrave.com/virtual-cemetery/359861.

"Dred Scott Died September 17, 1858. ." Biography.com. A&E Networks Television, May 12, 2021. https://www.biography.com/activist/dred-scott.

Ecelbarger, Gary, ed. "John A. Logan. He Won Three More U.S. House Elections (1866, 1868, 1870) and as a Republican and an Advocate of African American Civil Rights." Encyclopædia Britannica. Encyclopædia Britannica, inc. Accessed June 26, 2022. https://www.britannica.com/biography/John-A-Logan.

Editors of Encyclopaedia, Britannica, T. "William McKinley_biography." Encyclopædia Britannica. Encyclopædia Britannica, inc. Accessed May 28, 2022. https://www.britannica.com/biography/William-McKinley.

Editors of Encyclopaedia., Britannica, T. "Calvin Coolidge." Encyclopædia Britannica. Encyclopædia Britannica, inc. Accessed June 3, 2022. https://www.britannica.com/biography/Calvin-Coolidge.

Editors of Encyclopaedia., Britannica, T. "William McKinley Was Born January 29, 1843." Encyclopædia Britannica. Encyclopædia Britannica, inc. Accessed May 30, 2022. https://www.britannica.com/biography/William-McKinley.

"Election of 1860." National Parks Service. U.S. Department of the Interior, November 4, 2016. https://www.nps.gov/subjects/inauguration/election-of-1860.htm.

"Elliott Bulloch Roosevelt." Everipedia.org. Everipedia Internationa. Accessed June 5, 2022. https://everipedia.org/Elliott_Bulloch_Roosevelt.

Ellis, J. J. "Thomas Jefferson/Biography." Encyclopædia Britannica. Encyclopædia Britannica, inc. Accessed May 28, 2022. https://www.britannica.com/biography/Thomas-Jefferson.

"Emancipation Proclamation (1863)." National Archives and Records Administration. National Archives and Records Administration. Accessed June 1, 2022. https://www.archives.gov/milestone-documents/emancipation-proclamation.

"The Emancipation Proclamation." National Archives and Records Administration. National Archives and Records Administration, January 28, 2022. https://www.archives.gov/exhibits/featured-documents/emancipation-proclamation.

"The Enslaved Households of President Zachary Taylor He Was Still against the Spread of Slavery to New US Territories of the United States." WHHA (en-US), December 9, 2019. https://www.whitehousehistory.org/the-enslaved-households-of-president-zachary-taylor.

Estibillo, Nemecia." The Indians Were Ultimately Repulsed When Their Ammunition Ran Low." What was the final event of the Battle of Tippecanoe? AskingLot.com LTD, January 31, 2020. https://askinglot.com/whatwas-the-final-event-of-the-battle-of-tippecanoe.

Evans, Karen. "Would Learn the Strength and Position of British Units and Their Plan to Attack." Tribute to Veterans. July 4, 2016. https://evanskaren.wordpress.com/2016/07/04/birth-of-an-anthem/.

"February 9, 1775, Parliament Declared Massachusetts to Be in a Stage of Rebellion." National Parks Service. U.S. Department of the Interior. Accessed June 8, 2022.

https://www.nps.gov/waro/learn/historyculture/timeline-of-the-war-for-independence.htm.

"The Federalist Papers - Crf-Usa.org." Constitutional Rights Foundation. Accessed June 4, 2022. https://www.crfusa.org/images/pdf/Federalist%20Papers.pdf.

"The Federalist Papers." Wikipedia. Wikimedia Foundation, May 31, 2022. https://en.wikipedia.org/wiki/The_Federalist_Papers.

"First Battle of Bull Run Winfield Scott Laid out His Strategy to Subdue the Confederate States." Wikipedia. Wikimedia Foundation, July 15, 2022. https://en.wikipedia.org/wiki/First_Battle_of_Bull_Run.

"First Public Reading of The Declaration of Independence." National Parks Service. U.S. Department of the Interior. Accessed June 3, 2022. https://www.nps.gov/inde/learn/news/first-public-reading-of-the-declaration-of-independence.htm.

Flook, Contributor: Jim. "Confederate President Jefferson Davis Was Captured May 10, 1865." Encyclopedia Virginia. Virginia Humanities, December 14, 2020. https://encyclopediavirginia.org/entries/jefferson-davissimprisonment/.

Fraga, Kaleena. "The Short, Inspiring Life of Quentin Roosevelt, the Only American President's Son to Ever Be Killed in Combat." All That's Interesting. All That's Interesting, March 16, 2022. https://allthatsinteresting.com/quentin-roosevelt.

"Frances Cleveland." Wikipedia. Wikimedia Foundation, June 21, 2022. https://en.wikipedia.org/wiki/Frances_Cleveland.

"Frances Wright." History of American Women, May 23, 2020. https://www.womenhistoryblog.com/2012/01/frances-wright.html.

"Frances-Wright Met with James Madison, James Monroe, and Thomas Jefferson." Encyclopedia.com. Encyclopedia.com, May 30, 2022. https://www.encyclopedia.com/people/social-sciences-and-law/social-reformers/frances-wright.

"Fredrick Douglass Escapes Slavery," Biography.com (A&E Networks Television, July 15, 2021), https://www.biography.com/activists/frederickdouglass.

Freidel, F. "Franklin D. Roosevelt." Encyclopædia Britannica. Encyclopædia Britannica, inc. Accessed June 8, 2022. https://www.britannica.com/biography/Franklin-D-Roosevelt.

"Fundamentally Built on a Tyranny of Aristocracy and Monarchy." George Washington's Mount Vernon. Mount Vernon Ladies' Association., October 18, 2018. https://www.mountvernon.org/library/digitalhistory/digital-encyclopedia/article/thomas-paine/.

"George Eacker Died January 4, 1804 ." Find a Grave. Accessed May 30, 2022. https://www.findagrave.com/memorial/12683634/george-i-eacker.

"George Washington Adams." geni_family_tree, April 29, 2022. https://www.geni.com/people/George-Adams/600000000351068345.

"George Washington and His Wife and Her Children." Ancestors of Margaret Lillian Clark Martha Dandridge Custis. Millennia, June 11, 2014. http://bigfish153.50webs.com/our%20big%20family%20tree/2259.htm.

"George Washington and the Constitution." Center for the Study of the American Constitution. The University of Wisconsin System. Accessed May 28, 2022. https://csac.history.wisc.edu/document-collections/george-washington-and-the-constitution/.

"George Washington Parke Custis Daughter Married Robert E Lee." National Parks Service. U.S. Department of the Interior, August 6, 2020. https://www.nps.gov/arho/learn/historyculture/george-custis.htm.

"George Washington Parke Custis." Wikipedia. Wikimedia Foundation, May 22, 2022. https://en.wikipedia.org/wiki/George_Washington_Parke_Custis.

"George Washington Received a Note concerning Lafayette's Plan to End Slavery." George Washington's Mount Vernon. Accessed May 29, 2022. https://www.mountvernon.org/library/digitalhistory/digitalencyclopedia/article/marquis-de-lafayette-s-plan-for-slavery/.

"George Washington Was the Highest Ranked General of the Continental Army His Title Was General and Commander in Chief of the Continental

Army." Biography.com. A&E Networks Television, September 11, 2020. https://www.biography.com/us-president/george-washington.

"Gerald Ford, a Lieutenant Commander in the Navy." The White House. The United States Government, January 18, 2021. https://www.white-house.gov/about-the-white-house/presidents/gerald-r-ford/.

"Gettysburg Casualties: The Bloodiest Civil War Battle." History. HistoryOnTheNet, May 28, 2020. https://www.historyonthenet.com/gettysburgcasualties-bloodiest-civil-war-battle.

Giacalone, Joe, Mia L., Gucci God 69, K Hoeft, AG from MD, Bruce Hillman, Mary Rose Francini, et al. "Maryland Becomes Seventh U.S. State." Mystic Stamp Discovery Center, April 28, 2022. https://info.mysticstamp.com/this-day-in-history-april-28-1788/.

"Gilbert Du Motier, Marquis De Lafayette and His Battles." Wikipedia. Wikimedia Foundation, April 22, 2022. https://en.wikipedia.org/wiki/Gilbert_du_Motier,_Marquis_de_Lafayette.

Glad, Paul W. "William McKinley Served in the Civil War That Preserved the Union That Ended Involuntary Servitude." Encyclopedia.com. Encyclopedia.com, May 14, 2018. https://www.encyclopedia.com/people/history/us-history-biographies/william-mckinley.

Glass, Andrew. "American Troops Raise U.S. Flag in Puerto Rico, Oct. 18, 1898." POLITICO. POLITICO LLC, February 3, 2020. https://www.politico.com/story/2018/10/18/american-troops-raise-us-flag-in-puerto-ricooct-18-1898-898937.

Glass, Andrew. "Lincoln Memorial Dedicated, May 30, 1922." POLITICO. POLITICO. LCC, May 29, 2016. https://www.politico.com/story/2016/05/lincoln-memorial-dedicated-may30-1922-223676.

Glass, Andrew. "Revolutionary War Ends April 15, 1783." POLITICO. POLITICO LLC, February 3, 2020. https://www.politico.com/story/2008/04/revolutionary-war-ends-april-151783-009589.

Glass, Andrew. "Truman Ends Racial Segregation in Armed Forces, July 26, 1948, and Defense Secretary Robert McNamara Instructed Military Commanders to Boycott." POLITICO, July 26, 2018. https://www.politico.com/story/2018/07/26/this-day-in-politics-july-26-1948-735081.

"Gouverneur Morris Spoke Openly against Slavery ." Wikipedia. Wikimedia Foundation, June 5, 2022. https://en.wikipedia.org/wiki/Gouverneur_Morris.

"Grace Anna Goodhue Coolidge (1879-1957) - Find a..." Find a Grave. Accessed June 3, 2022. https://www.findagrave.com/memorial/8622/graceanna-coolidge.

"Grave of George Brinski." Polonia Trail. Polonia Trail | Polish-American Congress WNY. Accessed August 4, 2022. https://poloniatrail.com/location/grave-george-brinski/.

"Hamilton-Eacker Duel Four Months Later." Hamilton Wiki. Fandom, Inc., August 11, 2022. https://hamiltonmusical.fandom.com/wiki/HamiltonEacker_duel.

"Hannibal Hamlin Died July 4, 1891." geni_family_tree. Geni.com, April 28, 2022. https://www.geni.com/people/Hannibal-Hamlin-15th-Vice-President-of-the-USA/6000000001273541411.

Hardin County, Ohio, Kenton. "Jacob Parrott: U.S. Civil War: U.S. Army: Medal of Honor Recipient." Congressional Medal of Honor Society. CONGRESSIONAL MEDAL OF HONOR SOCIETY, June 16, 2021. https://www.cmohs.org/recipients/jacob-parrott.

Hardy, Michael C. "McClellan's Missed Opportunity." HistoryNet, November 21, 2018. https://www.historynet.com/mcclellans-missed-opportunity/.

"Harrison Camped near Prophetstown on November 6 and Arranged to Meet with Tenskwatawa." Wikipedia. Wikimedia Foundation, June 6, 2022. https://en.wikipedia.org/wiki/Battle_of_Tippecanoe.

Haynes, Michael. "Supreme Commander of the Allied Forces - Dwight D. Eisenhower." BUSINESS & LEADERSHIP, May 26, 2019.

https://www.businessandleadership.com/leadership/item/dwight-d-eisenhower-allied-forces-supreme-commander/.

"Helena, Mother of Constantine Was Greek." Wikipedia. Wikimedia Foundation, June 19, 2022. https://en.wikipedia.org/wiki/Helena,_mother_of_Constantine_I.

Henry, N. L.. "Freeed Enslaved Africans in the Caribbean and South Africa." Encyclopædia Britannica. Encyclopædia Britannica, inc. Accessed June 11, 2022. https://www.britannica.com/topic/Slavery-Abolition-Act.

Hickman, Kennedy. "Having Captured New Orleans and Memphis in Early 1862, Confederacy in Split the Confederacy into Half Two." ThoughtCo, October 17, 2019. https://www.thoughtco.com/siege-of-porthudson-2360954.

Hickman, Kennedy. "First Blood in Vietnam: Battle of Ia Drang." ThoughtCo. ThoughtCo, October 3, 2019. https://www.thoughtco.com/vietnam-war-battle-of-ia-drang-2361340.

History.com Editors, ed. "First Enslaved Africans Arrive in Jamestown Colony." History.com, March 16, 2021. https://www.history.com/this-day-in-history/first-african-slave-ship-arrives-jamestown-colony.

History.com Editors, ed. "Adolf Hitler Commits Suicide." History.com. A&E Television Networks, April 27, 2022. https://www.history.com/thisday-in-history/adolf-hitler-commits-suicide.

History.com Editors, ed. "Civil Rights Act of 1964 Signed July 2." History.com. A&E Television Networks, June 28, 2022. https://www.history.com/this-day-in-history/johnson-signs-civil-rights-act.

History.com Editors, ed. "Thomas Paine Publishes 'Common Sense' January 9, 1776." History.com. A&E Television Networks, January 7, 2020. https://www.history.com/this-day-in-history/thomas-paine-publishes-common-sense.

History.com Editors. "19th Amendment -James R. Mann and When Tennessee Voted on August 18, 1920., Definition, Passage & Summary." History.com, March 9, 2022. https://www.history.com/topics/womens-history/19th-amendment-1.

History.com Editors. "Battle of Antietam ." History.com. A&E Television Networks, October 15, 2009. https://www.history.com/topics/american-civil-war/american-civil-war-history.

History.com Editors. "Gerald Ford Was Born in Omaha, Nebraska, July 14, 1913." History.com. A&E Television Networks, March 15, 2022. https://www.history.com/topics/us-presidents/gerald-r-ford.

History.com Editors. "Americans Defeat the British at Yorktown." History.com. A&E Television Networks, October 20, 2021. https://www.history.com/this-day-in-history/victory-at-yorktown.

History.com Editors. "First Battle of Bull Run." History.com. A&E Television Networks, December 11, 2019. https://www.history.com/topics/american-civil-war/first-battle-of-bull-run.

History.com Editors. "First Battle of Bull RunMcDowell Had to Prepare a Command 35,000 Union Volunteers and Pushed for a Suspension to Give Him Time for Further Training. But Lincoln Ordered Him to Begin the Offensive." History.com. A&E Television Networks, April 1, 2011. https://www.history.com/topics/american-civil-war/first-battle-of-bull-run.

History.com Editors. "Former President Taft Dedicates Lincoln Memorial." History.com. A&E Television Networks, May 25, 2022. https://www.history.com/this-day-in-history/former-president-taft-dedicates-lincoln-memorial.

History.com Editors. "Fort Sumter 86 Soldiers." History.com. A&E Television Networks, December 11, 2019. https://www.history.com/topics/american-civil-war/fort-sumter.

History.com Editors. "France Gives The Statue of Liberty to the United States." History.com. A&E Television Networks, June 28, 2019. https://www.history.com/this-day-in-history/france-gives-statue-of-libertyto-united-states-friendship.

History.com Editors. "George Washington Is Born." History.com. A&E Television Networks, February 23, 2022. https://www.history.com/this-dayin-history/george-washington-is-born.

History.com Editors. "Island Fortification of Fort Sumter ." History.com. A&E Television Networks, December 11, 2019. https://www.history.com/topics/american-civil-war/fort-sumter.

History.com Editors. "John F. Kennedy Berlin Wall." History.com. A&E Television Networks, June 24, 2021. https://www.history.com/this-day-inhistory/kennedy-claims-solidarity-with-the-people-of-berlin.

History.com Editors. "John Tyler Elected to the Confederate House of Representatives." History.com. A&E Television Networks, January 27, 2022. https://www.history.com/topics/us-presidents/john-tyler.

History.com Editors. "Juneteenth Celebrated." History.com. A&E Television Networks, June 15, 2022. https://www.history.com/this-day-in-history/abolition-of-slavery-announced-in-texas-juneteenth.

History.com Editors. "Robert E. Lee Surrenders." History.com. A&E Television Networks, April 28, 2022. https://www.history.com/this-day-in-history/robert-e-lee-surrenders.

History.com Editors. "Treaty of Paris, Date - signed by Franklin, Adams, and Jay," November 13, 2009. https://www.history.com/topics/american-revolution/treaty-of-paris

History.com Editors. "U.S. Entry into World War I Germany's U-Boat Submarine Warfare Resumes The Zimmerman Telegram." History.com. A&E Television Networks, July 22, 2020. https://www.history.com/topics/world-war-i/u-s-entry-into-world-war-i-1.

History.com Editors. "War of 1812." History.com. A&E Television Networks, October 6, 2021. https://www.history.com/topics/war-of-1812/war-of-1812.

History.com Editors. "When John F. Kennedy Died." History.com. A&E Television Networks, June 5, 2022. https://www.history.com/topics/us-presidents/john-f-kennedy.

"History: Missouri Compromise." Murrell Library Research Guides. Missouri Valley College, March 10, 2022. https://libguides.moval.edu/c.php?g=957376&p=7041623.

Hoekstra, Kyle. "Lee Harvey Oswald, Was Born October 18, 1939." History Hit. History Hit, November 18, 2021. https://www.historyhit.com/facts-about-lee-harvey-oswald/.

Hogan, Margaret A., Margaret A. Hogan Former Managing Editor, Margaret A. Hogan, and Former Managing Editor. "John Quincy Adams: Life after the Presidency." Miller Center. Rector and Visitors of the University of Virginia, June 20, 2017. https://millercenter.org/president/jqadams/lifeafter-the-presidency.

Hunter, Hannah - Russell. "July 21, 1656: Elizabeth Key Wins Her Freedom." Zinn Education Project, July 22, 2023. https://www.zinnedproject.org/news/tdih/elizabeth-key-wins-freedom/.

IFHC4Idaho, Written by. "The Civil War Was Officially Over. May 9, 1865." Intermountain Fair Housing Council, October 27, 2021. https://ifhcidaho.org/timeline/may-9-1865-an-end-to-the-civil-war/.

"Inauguration of William Henry Harrison." Wikipedia. Wikimedia Foundation, December 8, 2021. https://en.wikipedia.org/wiki/Inauguration_of_William_Henry_Harrison.

"Intended to Run as a Federalist." Election of 1804. Accessed May 28, 2022. https://www.monticello.org/site/research-and-collections/election1804.

Intergrid. cat. "Killing of Archduke Franz Ferdinand and His Wife Sophie." La vaca cega desconfiada. Accessed July 3, 2022. https://www.histo.cat/premsa/Killing-of-Archduke-Franz-Ferdinand-andhis-wife-Sophie-.

"James A. Garfield Took Place in Washington, D.C. on July 2, 1881, at the Baltimore and Potomac Railroad Station." US President James Garfield (aged 49) was shot by Charles Guiteau in Washington, DC. Nekropole Info. Accessed June 30, 2022. http://placenote.info/en/events/US-President-James-Garfield-(aged-49)was-shot-by-Charles-Guiteau-in-Washington-DC.

"James Madison Proposes the Bill of Rights, on This Day in History, June 8, 1789." Revolutionary War and Beyond. Accessed May 28, 2022. https://www.revolutionary-war-and-beyond.com/james-madison-proposesbill-of-rights.html.

James. "How Did World War 1 Start?" Primary Facts, September 28, 2016. https://primaryfacts.com/4843/how-did-world-war-1-start.

"James Wilson (Founding Father) The Three Fifth Act." Wikipedia, December 3, 2023. https://en.wikipedia.org/wiki/James_Wilson_(Founding_Father).

"Jefferson Davis - Provisional President." Mr. Nussbaum - Jefferson Davis - President of the Confederacy. MrNussbaum.com is a copyright of the Nussbaum Education Network, LLC. Accessed June 9, 2022. https://mrnussbaum.com/jefferson-davis.

"Jefferson Davis and Abraham Lincoln: Contrasts North and South - Kentucky." Accessed June 1, 2022. https://www.sos.ky.gov/land/resources/articles/Documents/JDandAL.pdf.

Jefferson, Thomas. "Text of the Declaration of Independence." Encyclopædia Britannica. Encyclopædia Britannica, inc. Accessed June 1, 2022. https://www.britannica.com/topic/Declaration-of-Independence/Text-ofthe-Declaration-of-Independence.

"John Adams II." prabook.com. Prabook is a registered trademark of World Biographical Encyclopedia, Inc. Accessed June 12, 2022. https://prabook.com/web/john.adams_ii/2235049.

"John Alexander Logan, 1826-1886Logan Worked to Defeat a Bill Granting Blacks the Right to Testify in Court." SCRC Virtual Museum at Southern Illinois University's Morris Library. Accessed June 26, 2022. https://scrcexhibits.omeka.net/exhibits/show/sihistory/poststatehood/logan.

"John Hancock, Signer of the 'Declaration of Independence.'" geni_family_tree. Geni.com, April 26, 2022. https://www.geni.com/people/John-Hancock-Signer-of-the-Declaration-ofIndependence/6000000002504108 92.

"John Hanson - One of America's Founding Fathers November 5, 1781 John Hansen Elected the Articles of Confederation." The Constitutional Walking Tour of Philadelphia. The Constitutional Walking Tour of Philadelphia, December 30, 2020.

https://www.theconstitutional.com/blog/2020/12/30/john-hanson-oneamericas-founding-fathers.

“John Parke Custis November 5, 1781.” Wikipedia. Wikimedia Foundation, June 27, 2022. https://en.wikipedia.org/wiki/John_Parke_Custis.

“John Parker – September 17, 1775).” Military Wiki. Accessed June 12, 2022. https://military-history.fandom.com/wiki/John_Parker_(captain).

“John Quincy Adams and the Whig party.” Wikipedia, December 19, 2023. https://en.wikipedia.org/wiki/John_Quincy_Adams.

“John Quincy Adams Had Three Sons.” Critics Rant | Ranting on Pop Culture, Product Reviews, Tech, and More. Critics rant, May 16, 2022. https://criticsrant.com/the-children-of-john-quincy-adams/.

“Joseph Pannell Taylor.” Wikipedia. Wikimedia Foundation, July 27, 2022. https://en.wikipedia.org/wiki/Joseph_Pannell_Taylor.

“The Kansas Nebraska Act Passed May 30th, 1854.” The history place - abraham lincoln: Kansas-Nebraska Act. The history place. Accessed May 30, 2022. https://www.historyplace.com/lincoln/kansas.htm.

“Katherine McKinley Died June 25, 1875.” Answers. Answers Corporation. Accessed June 27, 2022. https://www.answers.com/Q/Who_were_William_McKinley's_children.

Keating, Dennis W. “Presidents Who Were Civil War Veterans.” William Mckinley served under Rutherford B Hayes. Virginia Center for Civil War Studies at Virginia Tech. Accessed May 29, 2022. https://www.essentialcivilwarcurriculum.com/presidents-who-were-civil-war-veterans.html.

Kelly, Martin. “a Professor at the College of New Jersey in 1890... and a Student in 1875.” ThoughtCo. ThoughtCo, June 5, 2019. https://www.thoughtco.com/woodrow-wilson-fast-facts-105510.

Kelsy PetersonFollowManages overall online presence and content initiatives., and Kelsy Peterson. “Ever Wonder Why Those Four Faces Made Mount Rushmore?” VisitRapidCity.com, July 8, 2021. https://www.visitrapidcity.com/blog/2021/07/ever-wonder-why-those-four-faces-made-mount-rushmore.

"Kentucky's Bloodiest Civil War Battle - Perryville." Middle Creek. Middle Creek National Battlefield, May 21, 2020. https://www.middlecreek.org/kentuckys-bloodiest-civil-war-battle-perryville/.

Kettler, Sara. "Who Was Hitler's Mother?" Biography.com. A&E Networks Television, June 15, 2020. https://www.biography.com/news/who-was-hitlers-mother.

Khomina, Anna. "Ulysses S. Grant Died July 23, 1885. ." Ulysses S. Grant Dies: On This Day, July 23, 1885, | Gilder Lehrman Institute of American History, July 23, 2017. https://www.gilderlehrman.org/news/ulysses-s-grantdies-day-july-23-1885.

Kirst, Sean, Courtesy of Barbara Seals Nevergold, Harry Scull Jr., and Sharon Cantillon. "Column: Reclaiming a Hero Who Tried to Save President McKinley." Buffalo News, February 12, 2021. https://buffalonews.com/opinion/columnists/column-reclaiming-a-herowho-tried-to-save-president-mckinley/article_d8de4844-eeb3-11ea-a8b153d3e8221da4.html.

Klos, Stanley Yavneh, and Naomi Klos. President Peyton Randolph, January 1, 1970. https://www.peytonrandolph.com/.

Koutsoubos, Doumbia. "The British Attack at Fort McHenry with Nineteen Ships." Who saw the British attack on Fort McHenry from Baltimore Harbor? AskingLot.com, March 9, 2020. https://askinglot.com/who-saw-thebritish-attack-of-fort-mchenry-from-baltimore-harbor.

Kunze, Stefanie. "Stamp Act of 1765." Stamp Act of 1765. John Seigenthaler Chair of Excellence in First Amendment Studies. Accessed June 13, 2022. https://mtsu.edu/first-amendment/article/1035/stamp-act-of1765.

"Lafayette Decided to Purchase a Plantation in the French Colony of Cayenne." Lafayette Society. Lafayette Society, June 15, 2018. https://www.lafayettesociety.org/lafayette-and-slavery/.

Landy Author Historical Society of the New York Courts, Craig, A. "When Did Slavery End in New York?" Historical Society of the New York

Courts, October 24, 2018. https://history.nycourts.gov/when-did-slavery-end-innew-york/.

"The Last Viceroy of New Spain, Juan O'Donojú, Died of Pleurisy Shortly after Independence on October 8, 1821, Just Two and a Half Months after Arriving in New Spain." Reddit. Accessed June 2, 2022. https://www.reddit.com/r/200YearsAgo/comments/q3xcpf/the_last_viceroy_of_new_spain_juan_odonoj%C3%BA_died/.

Le Barbier, Jean Jacques-Francois. "Lafayette's Draft of the Declaration of the Rights of Man and the Citizen." American Battlefield Trust. Accessed May 29, 2022. https://www.battlefields.org/learn/primary-sources/lafayettes-draft-declaration-rights-man-and-citizen.

Lewis, J.D. "Only One Patriot Died." North Carolina early statehood - the battle of Moore's creek. Accessed September 17, 2023. https://www.carolana.com/NC/Revolution/revolution_battle_of_moores_creek.html.

Lillback, Peter. "Decoration Day May 30, 1868, for 20,000 Union and Confederate Soldiers Buried at Arlington National Cemetery." Fox News. FOX News Network, May 29, 2017. https://www.foxnews.com/opinion/why-thisspeech-from-the-first-memorial-day-still-resonates-today.

"Lincoln Called for Volunteer Militia to Overthrow the Rebellion." HistoryNet. HistoryNet., August 9, 2012. https://www.historynet.com/confederacy/.

"Lincoln on Slavery." National Parks Service. U.S. Department of the Interior. Accessed May 28, 2022. https://www.nps.gov/liho/learn/historyculture/slavery.htm.

"Lincoln Was Present When Congressman and Former President John Quincy Adams Collapsed on the House Floor." Abraham Lincoln and the U.S. capitol. Abraham Lincoln Online. Accessed June 12, 2022. http://www.abrahamlincolnonline.org/lincoln/sites/uscapitol.htm.

Lincoln, Abraham. "Abraham Lincoln's Lost Speech." The Project Gutenberg eBook of Lincoln's Lost Speech, by Abraham Lincoln. gutenberg.org, April 28, 2020.

https://www.gutenberg.org/files/61966/61966-h/61966h.htm.

Lincoln, Abraham. "February 11, 1861: Farewell Address." Miller Center, February 23, 2017. https://millercenter.org/the presidency/presidential-speeches/february-11- 1861-farewell-address. -

"Lincoln's Second Inaugural Address." National Parks Service. U.S. Department of the Interior. Accessed June 12, 2022. https://www.nps.gov/linc/learn/historyculture/lincoln-secondinaugural.htm.

lithographer. Currier & Ives. "The Battle of Buena Vista 1847." The battle of buena vista. Library of Congress. Accessed June 25, 2022. https://www.americaslibrary.gov/jb/reform/jb_reform_buena_1.html.

"Logan Was Replaced as Corps Commander by Major General O.O. Howard, a Decision Made by Major General William T. Sherman Because of Sherman's Mistrust of 'Political' Generals." The Campaign for the National Museum of the United States Army. The Army Historical Foundation. Accessed June 26, 2022. https://armyhistory.org/general-john-a-logan-memorial-day-founder/.

Lohnes, K. "Battles of Saratoga." Encyclopedia Britannica, September 12, 2023. https://www.britannica.com/event/Battles-of-Saratoga.

Lowe Qiu, Danielle, Marissa Jeung, and Hai Long. "One of Wilson's Fourteen Points Was Carried out and Accepted. This Point That They Had Accepted Was the League of Nations." World War II. powered by Weebly. Accessed July 2, 2022. https://worldwar2wasnecessary.weebly.com/the-treaty-of-versailles.html.

"Lyndon B Johnson Signed Voting Rights Act of 1965 (U.S. National Park Service)." National Parks Service. U.S. Department of the Interior. Accessed August 3, 2022. https://www.nps.gov/articles/votingrightsact.htm.

M.D., Robert H. Johnson, Sheri McKnight, Duke Kraus, Miks Short, Nita, Steve Byrd, Stuart Clarke, et al. "September 15 — 16, 1810, Hidalgo Declared War on the Colonial Government in What Has Been Named the Cry of Dolores." Mystic Stamp Discovery Center, June 21, 2021. https://info.mysticstamp.com/this-day-in-history-september-27-1821/.

M.D., Robert H. Johnson, Sheri McKnight, Duke Kraus, Miks Short, Nita, Steve Byrd, Stuart Clarke, et al. "Mexico Gains Independence from Spain." Mystic Stamp Discovery Center, June 21, 2021. https://info.mysticstamp.com/this-day-in-history-september-27-1821/.

M.D., Robert H. Johnson, Sheri McKnight, Duke Kraus, Miks Short, Nita, Steve Byrd, Stuart Clarke, et al. "Mexico Gains Independence from Spain." Mystic Stamp Discovery Center. Mystic Stamp Company, June 21, 2021. https://info.mysticstamp.com/this-day-in-history-september-27-1821/.

Magazine, Smithsonian. "Quentin Roosevelt s Plane Crashed Behind Enemy Lines on July 14, 1918." Smithsonian.com. Smithsonian Institution, April 3, 2017. https://www.smithsonianmag.com/smithsonian-institution/letters-unbearable-grief-theodore-roosevelt-death-son-180962743/.

Mandresh, Jason. "George Eacker - Two Duels in Two Days ." Founder of the Day. Founder of the Day, January 16, 2022. https://www.founderof-theday.com/founder-of-the-day/eacker.

Mandresh, Jason. "Who Was the Last Founding Father? Charles Carroll and James Madison." Founder of the Day. Founder of the Day, March 26, 2018. https://www.founderoftheday.com/founder-of-the-day/last-foundingfather.

Maranzani, Barbara. "… Aaron Burr Graduated at the Age of 16 Years Old from the College of New Jersey ." History.com. A&E Television Networks, July 10, 2018. https://www.history.com/news/burr-hamilton-duel-politicallegacy-died.

Maranzani, Barbara. "Alexander Hamilton and Aaron Burr Exchanged a Series of Letters." Biography.com. A&E Networks Television, June 25, 2020. https://www.biography.com/news/alexander-hamilton-aaron-burr-relationship-rivalry-duel.

"Martin Luther King, March 3 1962 Urged John F Kennedy to Select Thurgood Marshall to Fill a Vacant Seat in the Supreme Court. ." Martin Luther King Jr. | JFK Library. The U.S. National Archives and

Records Administration. Accessed June 30, 2022. https://www.jfklibrary.org/learn/education/students/leaders-in-the-strugglefor-civil-rights/martin-luther-king-jr.

"Mary Anna Custis Lee Died November 5, 1873." Wikipedia. Wikimedia Foundation, May 27, 2022. https://en.wikipedia.org/wiki/Mary_Anna_Custis_Lee.

Masur, Louis P. "The Battle for Freedom: Antietam and the Emancipation Proclamation." The Battle For Freedom: Antietam and the Emancipation Proclamation | Commentary | Civil War Monitor, September 17, 2012. https://www.civilwarmonitor.com/front-line/the-battle-for-freedom-antietam-and-the-emancipation-proclamation.

Matthews, J., and Nicol. "Constantine I Died May 22 337 A.D." Encyclopædia Britannica. Encyclopædia Britannica, inc., May 18, 2022. https://www.britannica.com/biography/Constantine-I-Roman-emperor.

McCullough, David. George Washington Adams. Accessed June 6, 2022. https://detskydomov.sk/encyklopedia/?pojem=George_Washington_Adams.

McDermott, Annette. "June 25, 1876, near the Little Big Horn River in Present-Day Montana." History.com. A&E Television Networks, February 27, 2018. https://www.history.com/news/little-bighorn-battle-facts-causes.

McGaughy, Contributor: J. Kent. "Richard Henry Lee Was Born on January 20, 1732, and Died June 19, 1794..." Encyclopedia Virginia, January 20, 1732. https://encyclopediavirginia.org/entries/lee-richard-henry-17321794/.

McNamara, Robert. "American Troops with More Milia Troops." ThoughtCo. ThoughtCo, January 9, 2020. https://www.thoughtco.com/defenders-saved-baltimore-september-1814-1773540.

"Memorial Day 1971 Became a Federal Holiday." Wikipedia, August 11, 2023. https://en.wikipedia.org/wiki/Memorial_Day.

"The Moore House Became a Point of Significance on October 18, 1781,

Washington and Cornwallis Focused on the Surrender Negotiations Taking Place at This House." Williamsburg Tours. Williamsburg Tours. Accessed June 27, 2022. http://williamsburgtours.com/archives/925.

Moore, John D. "Theodore Roosevelt Middle of Honor in 2001." GUY COUNSELING, December 1, 2021. https://guycounseling.com/theo-doreroosevelt-accomplishments/.

Morley, Jefferson. "Jan. 3, 1967: Jack Ruby, Killer of JFK's Assassin, Dies Just Weeks before Second Trial > JFK Facts." JFK Facts, January 4, 2014. https://jfkfacts.org/jan-3-1967-jack-ruby-killer-of-jfks-assassin-dies-justweeks-before-second-trial/.

"Mr. Antonucci, Is a 68-Year from the Garfield Heights Section of Cleveland." The New York Times. The New York Times, April 1, 1981. https://www.nytimes.com/1981/04/01/us/man-who-tackled-suspect-is-ill.html.

"National Anthem." NMAH | National Anthem civil war. Smithsonian Institution, January 10, 2020. https://amhistory.si.edu/starspangled-banner/national-anthem.aspx.

"The National Woman Suffrage Association Was Created May 15, 1869 One of the Co-Founders Susan B Anthony." Wikipedia. Wikimedia Foundation, July 21, 2022.
https://en.wikipedia.org/wiki/National_Woman_Suffrage_Association.

NCC Staff. "Constitution Was Ratified June 21, 1788..." The National Constitution Center. National Constitution Center, June 21, 2021.
https://constitutioncenter.org/interactive-constitution/blog/the-day-thecon-stitution-was-ratified.

"Nellie Grant Was Born July 4, 1855." Critics Rant | Ranting on Pop Culture, Product Reviews, Tech, and More. https://criticsrant.com/affiliate-disclosure, May 2, 2022.
https://criticsrant.com/children-of-ulysses-s-grant/.

Nemy, Enid. "Betty Ford, Former First Lady, Dies at 93." The New York Times. The New York Times, July 9, 2011.
https://www.nytimes.com/2011/07/09/us/politics/betty-ford-dies.html.

Network, The Learning. "Jan. 6, 1919, | Theodore Roosevelt Dies." The New York Times. The New York Times, January 6, 2012. https://learning.blogs.nytimes.com/2012/01/06/jan-6-1919-theodore-roosevelt-dies/.

Neufeld, Rob. "The Battle of Palmito Ranch, Texas, May 12-13, 1865 ." The Asheville Citizen-Times, April 12, 2015. https://www.citizentimes.com/story/life/2015/04/12/visiting-past-confederacys-last-strategicvictory/25686179/.

"The New Electrical Process Was the First Used for the 1804 Election the Twelfth Amendment." Wikipedia. Wikimedia Foundation, May 1, 2022. https://en.wikipedia.org/wiki/Twelfth_Amendment_to_the_United_States_ Constitution.

"The New York Governor's Race Hamilton s Speech about Burr." PBS. Public Broadcasting Service. Accessed May 28, 2022. https://www.pbs.org/wgbh/americanexperience/features/duel-new-yorkgovernors-race/.

Newtonic, Learnodo, and Craig T. Eierman. "He Fought in the Battle of Carnifex Ferry and the Battle of Antietam." Learnodo Newtonic, November 12, 2019. https://learnodo-newtonic.com/william-mckinley-accomplishments.

Nicholas, H. G. "Winston Churchill." Encyclopædia Britannica. Encyclopædia Britannica, inc. Accessed June 11, 2022. https://www.britannica.com/biography/Winston-Churchill.

Oldham, Kit. Washington is admitted as the 42nd state to the United States of America on November 11, 1889. HistoryLink.org, March 1, 2022. https://www.historylink.org/File/5210.

Oliete, Oprea. "Hamilton Preferred Thomas Jefferson as President over Burr." Why did Hamilton Pick Jefferson over burr? AskingLot, July 1, 2020. https://askinglot.com/why-did-hamilton-pick-jefferson-over-burr.

"Olive Branch Petition." American Battlefield Trust. American Battlefield Trust. Accessed June 17, 2022. https://www.battlefields.org/learn/primarysources/olive-branch-petition.

"On February 21, 1848, John Quincy Suffered a Stroke, Fell to the Floor of the House, and Died Two Days Later in the Capitol Building." National Parks Service. U.S. Department of the Interior, February 15, 2022. https://www.nps.gov/adam/learn/historyculture/john-quincy-adams-17671848.htm.

"On His 32nd Day, He Became the First to Die in Office, Serving the Shortest." The White House. The United States Government, January 15, 2021. https://www.whitehouse.gov/about-the-white-house/presidents/william-henry-harrison/.

O'Neill, Aaron. "Of the First 12 Presidents John Adam and His Son Were the Only Two Presidents to Naver Own Slaves." Statista, June 21, 2022. https://www.statista.com/statistics/1121963/slaves-owned-by-us-presidents/.

"Parliament - an Act Repealing the Stamp Act; March 18, 1766." American Battlefield Trust. American Battlefield Trust, May 2022. https://www.battlefields.org/learn/primary-sources/parliament-act-repealing-stamp-actmarch-18-1766.

"Parliament Completes the Coercive Acts with the Quartering Act." History.com. A&E Television Networks, November 13, 2009. https://www.history.com/this-day-in-history/parliament-completes-the-coercive-acts-with-t he-quartering-act.

Past, Black B. "(1776) The Deleted Passage of the Declaration of Independence..." •Deleted anti-slavery passage in the Declaration of Independence. BlackPast.org., August 22, 2019. https://www.blackpast.org/african-american-history/declaration-independence-and-debate-over-slavery/.

"Patrick Henry - Give Me Liberty or Give Me Death March 23, 1775." geni_family_tree. Geni.com, April 28, 2022. https://www.geni.com/people/Patrick-Henry/6000000002746326589.

Peck, Graham A. "Stephen Douglas Introduced the Kansas and Nebraska January 4, 1854." Originals. Historical Research and Narrative. Accessed May 30, 2022. https://www.lib.niu.edu/2003/iht1010302.html.

Periodicpresidents. “Which Presidents Were Generals?” Periodic Presidents. Periodic Presidents, September 3, 2021. https://periodicpresidents.com/2014/10/15/which-presidents-were-generals/.

“Perryville.” American Battlefield Trust. American Battlefield Trust. Accessed June 1, 2022. https://www.battlefields.org/learn/civil-war/battles/perryville.

“Philip Hamilton (the Second) Named after Philip Hamilton.” Wikipedia. Wikimedia Foundation, May 7, 2022. https://en.wikipedia.org/wiki/Philip_Hamilton_(the_second).

“Philip Hamilton Died November 24, 1801.” AncientFaces. AncientFaces, Inc. Accessed June 5, 2022. https://www.ancientfaces.com/person/philiphamilton-birth-1782-death-1801/613239.

“Philip Hamilton the Second.” geni_family_tree. Geni.com, April 29, 2022. https://www.geni.com/people/Philip-Hamilton/6000000000954132164.

“Philip Schuyler/Alexander Hamilton’s Father-in-Law the 1791 Battle for New York’s Seats in the U.S. Senate.” PBS. Public Broadcasting Service. Accessed May 27, 2022. https://www.pbs.org/wgbh/americanexperience/features/duel-philip-schuyler/.

“Photo of Boston Corbett Icon of Person Boston Corbett Thomas H. ‘Boston’ Corbett (January 29, 1832.” Pantheon. Accessed June 27, 2022. https://pantheon.world/profile/person/Boston_Corbett/.

Phyllis C. Murray on July 6, 2012, 7:08 PM | Comments | var addthis_config = {“data_track_addressbar”: true}; “ Thompkins Made a Recommendation to the Legislature for an Abolition of Domestic Slavery in the State.” July 4, 1827: Slavery is abolished in New York - Phyllis C. Murray. Accessed June 19, 2022. http://educationupdate.com/phyllismurray/2012/07/july-4-1827-slavery-isabolished-in-new-york.html.

“Political Party Timeline: 1836-1864.” PBS. Accessed July 3, 2023. https://www.pbs.org/wgbh/americanexperience/features/lincolns-timeline/.

Ponder, Arlan. "Medal of Honor." > Air Combat Command > Display. Official United States Air Force Website, July 22, 2009. https://www.acc.af.mil/News/Features/Display/Article/204365/presidentlincoln-creates-medal-of-honor/.

Prahl, Amanda. "Biography of Dolley Madison, Bipartisan First Lady." ThoughtCo. ThoughtCo, April 15, 2019. https://www.thoughtco.com/dolley-madison-first-lady-4684348.

"Preliminary Emancipation Proclamation, 1862 - Archives." American Regionals. The U.S. National Archives and Records Administration, September 8, 2020. https://www.archives.gov/exhibits/american_originals_iv/sections/preliminary_emancipation_proclamation.html.

"President John F. Kennedy's Message to Congress June 19. 1963." National Archives and Records Administration. National Archives and Records Administration. Accessed July 16, 2022. https://www.archives.gov/legislative/ features/march-on-washington/kennedy.html.

Press, Associated. "Today in History: On March 4, 1865, Abraham Lincoln Was Inaugurated for a Second Term." fox43.com. WPMT, March 4, 2020. https://www.fox43.com/article/news/history/today-in-history-on-march-41865-abraham-lincoln-was-inaugurated-for-a-second-term/521-aedf25dd9553-42b4-8f15-5e12b87efd09.

"Princeton to Be Burr's Successor as President of the College." Wikipedia. Wikimedia Foundation, May 16, 2022. https://en.wikipedia.org/wiki/Esther_Edwards_Burr.

Pruitt, Sarah. "Why FDR Decided to Run for a Fourth Term despite Ill Health." History.com. A&E Television Networks, March 12, 2020. https://www.history.com/news/franklin-d-roosevelt-health-final-term.

Pyle, Howard. "Declaration of Independence Is Read to Troops in New York City - July 9, 1776." Revolutionary War and Beyond. Accessed June 5, 2022. https://www.revolutionary-war-and-beyond.com/declaration-of-independence-read-troops-new-york-city.html.

"Quentin Roosevelt II Died in a Plane Crash." geni_family_tree, April 26,

2022. https://www.geni.com/people/Quentin-Roosevelt-II/6000000003681283300.
"Quentin Roosevelt II Was the Namesake of His Uncle Quentin Roosevelt I," Wikipedia. Wikimedia Foundation, May 17, 2022. https://en.wikipedia.org/wiki/Quentin_Roosevelt_II.
"Quentin Roosevelt Was Born November 19, 1897, in Washington DC." Find a Grave. Find a Grave, December 31, 2000. https://www.findagrave.com/memorial/2686/quentin-roosevelt.
Rafferty, John P. "William Wilberforce." Encyclopædia Britannica. Encyclopædia Britannica, inc. Accessed June 3, 2022. https://www.britannica.com/biography/William-Wilberforce.
Rafuse, Contributor: Ethan S. "Jefferson Davis (1808–1889) /Jefferson Davis Birth." Encyclopedia Virginia, June 3, 1808. https://encyclopediavirginia.org/entries/davis-jefferson-1808-1889/.
Ravet, Serra. "Fort Ticonderoga Served as a Morale Booster." Why was the Battle of fort ticonderoga in 1777 important? AskingLot.com LTD, February 12, 2020. https://askinglot.com/why-was-the-battle-of-fort-ticonderoga1777-important.
Reed, Leslie. "Became One of the First White Officers to Command African-American Soldiers in the 10th Cavalry..." Nebraska Today | University of Nebraska–Lincoln. University of Nebraska–Lincoln, November 9, 2017. https://news.unl.edu/newsrooms/today/article/11-things-you-probablydidnt-know-about-john-j-pershing/.
"Regiment of Missouri Field Artillery." National Parks Service. U.S. Department of the Interior, March 4, 2021. https://www.nps.gov/people/harrys-truman.htm.
"Rev. Aaron Burr SR." geni_family_tree. Geni.com, April 27, 2022. https://www.geni.com/people/Rev-Aaron-Burr/6000000001362917056.
Rhp. "The Speech Where Adolf Hitler Declared War on the USA, 1941." Rare Historical Photos. Rare Historical Photos, November 24, 2021. https://rarehistoricalphotos.com/adolf-hitler-declaration-warusa-1941/.

"Richard Taylor (Confederate General)." Wikipedia. Wikimedia Foundation, May 24, 2022. https://en.wikipedia.org/wiki/Richard_Taylor_(Confederate_general).

"Richmond Virginia Became the Capital for the Confederacy..." Virginia Museum of History & Culture. Virginia Historical Society. Accessed June 1, 2022. https://virginiahistory.org/learn/why-richmond.

"Roger Sherman." Wikipedia. Wikimedia Foundation, June 5, 2022. https://en.wikipedia.org/wiki/Roger_Sherman.

Rosenwald, Michael S. "The Police Officer Who Arrested a President." The Washington Post. WP Company, December 17, 2018. https://www.washingtonpost.com/history/2018/12/16/police-officer-who-arrested-president/.

Ross., Tara. "Calvin Coolidge Jr." Taraross. Taraross, July 7, 2021. https://www.taraross.com/post/tdih-coolidge-jr.

Rust, Randal. "Saratoga Campaign, Summary, Facts, Significance, Revolutionary American Revolutionary War, Saratoga Campaign, John Burgoyne, Horatio Gates, Siege of Fort Ticonderoga, Battle of Hubbardston, Siege of Fort Stanwix, Battle of Bennington, Battle of Oriskany, Battle of Freeman's Farm, Battle of Bemis Heights, Battles of Saratoga. First Battle of Saratoga, Second Battle of Saratoga." American History Central, August 15, 2023. https://www.americanhistorycentral.com/entries/saratoga-campaign-1777/.

"Santa María–Calatrava Treaty." Wikipedia. Wikimedia Foundation, October 8, 2021. https://en.wikipedia.org/wiki/Santa_Mar%C3%ADa%E2%80%93Calatrava_Treaty.

"Sarah Knox Taylor Married Jefferson Davis." Wikipedia. Wikimedia Foundation, June 2, 2021. https://en.wikipedia.org/wiki/Sarah_Knox_Taylor.

"Sarah Lincoln Grigsby (U.S. National Park Service)." National Parks Service. U.S. Department of the Interior, January 12, 2022. https://www.nps.gov/people/sarah-lincoln-grigsby.htm.

"Saratoga." American Battlefield Trust. Accessed August 9, 2022. https://www.battlefields.org/learn/revolutionary-war/battles/saratoga.

Sawe, Benjamin Elisha. "James Abram Garfield – Birth and Death." WorldAtlas. WorldAtlas, March 22, 2019. https://www.worldatlas.com/articles/james-a-garfield-20th-u-spresident.html.

Scarinci, Donald, ed. "United States Constitution President Administration Will End at Noon on January 20." Constitutional Law Reporter. Scarinci Hollenbeck, LLC. Accessed June 19, 2022. https://constitutionallawreporter.com/amendment-20/.

Schultz, Angela Michelle. "Franklin D Roosevelt: 32nd President: Longest Serving." Location. Owlcation, April 14, 2022. https://owlcation.com/humanities/Franklin-D-Roosevelt-32nd-President.

Sears, Stephen W. "'The Roar and Rattle': McClellan's Missed Opportunities at Antietam." HistoryNet, March 30, 2016. https://www.historynet.com/the-roar-and-rattle-mcclellans-missed-opportunities-at-antietam/.

Seegmuellertom.seegmueller@albanyherald.com, Tom. "The 11th Hour of the 11th Day of the 11th Month ...5:45 A.m. on Nov. 11, 1918, an Armistice Was Signed." Albany Herald, December 16, 2021. https://www.albanyherald.com/features/the-11th-hour-of-the-11th-day-of-the-11th-month/article_8cdd4e30-2226-11eb-b28e-47bbddd59f58.html.

Sejarah, dalam Hari ini. "February 6, 1778: The Franco-American Alliance." Zona Perang - Prepare For Future War, February 6, 2022. https://www.zonaperang.com/february-6-1778-the-franco-american-alliance/.

"September 17, 1781, Washington Gave Lafayette Overall Command of American Forces." The American Friends of Lafayette - Timeline. The American Friends of Lafayette. Accessed May 29, 2022. https://friendsoflafayette.wildapricot.org/Timeline.

Sicard, Sarah. "How Veterans Day Was Founded In His Proclamation, Wilson Stated, Canada, England, and France Used the Date to Honor Their Veterans as well. France to This Day Calls." Military

Times. Military Times, October 13, 2020. https://www.militarytimes.com/militaryhonor/salute-veterans/2019/11/05/how-veterans-day-was-founded/.

"Siege of Vicksburg Cutting off the States of Arkansas, Louisiana, and Texas and Successfully Completed the Ananda." Wikipedia. Wikimedia Foundation, July 8, 2022. https://en.wikipedia.org/wiki/Siege_of_Vicksburg.

"The Site of the Last Surrender of a Major Confederate Army." Wikipedia. Wikimedia Foundation, May 23, 2022. https://en.wikipedia.org/wiki/Bennett_Place.

"Slave Trade: Joseph Bradley Varnum March 3 and Thomas Jefferson." Slave Trade: Joseph Bradley Varnum - Untold Lowell Stories: Black History - LibGuides at University of Massachusetts Lowell. Accessed May 28, 2022. https://libguides.uml.edu/c.php?g=1125577&p=8210377+Joseph+Bradley+Varnum+March+3%2C+1805+proposition.

Smentkowski, B. P. "Thurgood Marshall." Encyclopædia Britannica. Encyclopædia Britannica, inc., June 28, 2022. https://www.britannica.com/biography/Thurgood-Marshall.

Sparrow, Director, FDR Library., Paul M. "The 'Four Freedoms' Speech Remastered." National Archives and Records Administration. National Archives and Records Administration, January 6, 2016. https://fdr.blogs.archives.gov/2016/01/06/four_freedoms/.

"St. Helena, the Legend of the True Cross, and The Holy Sepulcher." The Holy Land Franciscan Pilgrimages, February 22, 2019. https://holylandpilgrimages.org/st-helena-the-legend-of-the-true-cross-and-theholy-sepulcher/.

Staff, Snopes. "Presidential 20-Year Death Curse." Snopes.com. Snopes Media Group Inc, October 30, 2000. https://www.snopes.com/fact-check/the-curse-of-tecumseh/.

"Star-Spangled Banner." Smithsonian Institution. National Museum of American History, Behring Center In cooperation with Public Inquiry

Services, Smithsonian Institution. Accessed June 3, 2022. https://www.si.edu/spotlight/flag-day/banner-facts.

"Star Spangled Banner." The Library of Congress On July 26, 1889, the Secretary of the Navy designated "The Star Spangled Banner" as the official tune to be played at raising the flag. Accessed March 4, 2024. https://www.loc.gov/item/ihas.200000017.

"The Star-Spangled Banner Woodrow Wilson Signed Order of the Star Spangle Banner in 1916." Wikipedia, February 24, 2024. https://en.wikipedia.org/wiki/The_Star-Spangled_Banner.

"Started to Rain and Continued for Most of the Night. Battle of Northpoint." National Parks Service. U.S. Department of the Interior, September 11, 2020. https://www.nps.gov/fomc/learn/historyculture/north-point-pt-2.htm.

"Stephen Douglas Died." American Battlefield Trust. American Battlefield Trust. Accessed June 1, 2022. https://www.battlefields.org/learn/biographies/stephen-douglas.

Strauss, Valerie. "Analysis | Why John Adams Saw July 2 as America's True Independence Day and John Adams Wrote to His Wife." The Washington Post. WP Company, November 30, 2021. https://www.washingtonpost.com/news/answer-sheet/wp/2017/07/02/whyjohn-adams-saw-july-2-as-americas-true-independence-day/.

Sysadmin. "Benjamin Lincoln's Sword." Smithsonian's History Explorer. Verizon Foundation, February 8, 2016. https://historyexplorer.si.edu/resource/benjamin-lincolns-sword.

"Tad Lincoln." Wikipedia. Wikimedia Foundation, May 31, 2022. https://en.wikipedia.org/wiki/Tad_Lincoln.

Tejvan, Pettinger. "Biography Thomas Jefferson." Biography Online. Oxford, Uk, October 22, 2019. https://www.biographyonline.net/thomas_jefferson.html.

"Theodore Roosevelt Jr. the Medal of Honor September 21, 1944." Find a Grave. Find a Grave, December 31, 2000.

https://www.findagrave.com/memorial/2144/theodore-roosevelt.
"Theodore Roosevelt Sr.." Wikipedia. Wikimedia Foundation, June 7, 2022. https://en.wikipedia.org/wiki/Theodore_Roosevelt_Sr.

"Thomas Hickey (Soldier)." Wikipedia. Wikimedia Foundation, June 29, 2022. https://en.wikipedia.org/wiki/Thomas_Hickey_(soldier).

"Thomas Jefferson Fell into Depression When His Wife Martha Jefferson Die." geni_family_tree, April 27, 2022. https://www.geni.com/people/MarthaJefferson/6000000006597668288.

"Thomas Lincoln." geni_family_tree. Geni.com, April 26, 2022. https://www.geni.com/people/ThomasLincoln/4265729635020041688.

"Thomas Paine, 'African Slavery in America,' 1775." Bill of Rights Institute. Accessed September 17, 2023. https://www.billofrightsinstitute.org/activities/thomas-paine-african-slavery-in-america-1775.

"Thomas Paine Arrived in America with a Recommendation from Benjamin Franklin, November 30, 1774." MR. Nussbaum Learning and Fun Thomas Paine and Common Sense Reading Comprehension. MR. Nussbaum Learning and fun. Accessed June 12, 2022. https://mrnussbaum.com/uploads/activities/paine/paine.pdf.

Thomas Paine: African slavery in America. Accessed December 21, 2023. https://constitution.org/2-Authors/tp/afri.htm.

"Thomas Paine." Wikipedia. Wikimedia Foundation, June 4, 2022. https://en.wikipedia.org/wiki/Thomas_Paine.

Tikkanen, Amy. "Jack Ruby s Birth Date Is Uncertain, Though He Typically Used March 25, 1911." Encyclopædia Britannica. Encyclopædia Britannica, inc. Accessed June 27, 2022. https://www.britannica.com/biography/Jack-Ruby.

Timmons, Greg. "John Brown's Raid on Harpers Ferry." Biography.com. A&E Networks Television, October 2, 2020. Https://www.biography.com/news/john-brown-biography-harpers-ferry-raid.

"Today in History - April 30." The Library of Congress. Cungress.Gov. Accessed June 6, 2022. https://www.loc.gov/item/today-in-history/april-30.

"Today in History - Memorial Day May 30, 1868." Super Sabre Society. Super Sabre Society, May 10, 2021. https://supersabresociety.com/this_time_in_history/today-in-history-memorial-day-may-30-1868/.

"The Triumph and Tragedy of Franklin Pierce." New England Historical Society. New England Historical Society New England Historical Society, January 18, 2021. https://www.newenglandhistoricalsociety.com/triumphtragedy-franklin-pierce/.

"Two Presidents That Naver Owned Slaves." Wikipedia. Wikimedia Foundation, May 25, 2022. https://en.wikipedia.org/wiki/List_of_presidents_of_the_United_States_wh o_owned_slaves.

Tristan, David. "May 9, 1865: Civil War Declared 'Virtually over,' but Not Quite." ABC27, May 9, 2022. https://www.abc27.com/digital-originals/may-9-1865-civil-war-declared-virtually-over-but-not-quite/.

"U.S. Declares War on Germany..." www.army.mil. Accessed July 9, 2022. https://www.army.mil/article/7916/u_s_declares_war_on_germany.

"Ulysses S Grant Was the Supreme Union General." WhatisAny. Accessed June 30, 2022. http://ing.scottexteriors.com/who-was-better-robert-e-leeor-ulysses-s-grant/.

"Ulysses Simpson Grant Was Born July 4, 1881." Wikipedia. Wikimedia Foundation, March 11, 2022. https://en.wikipedia.org/wiki/Ulysses_S._Grant_III.

"Unit 3 Flashcards | Quizlet." Accessed June 14, 2022. https://quizlet.com/191421409/unit-3-flash-cards/.

Urofsky, M. I. "That a Slave (Dred Scott) Who Had Resided in a Free State and Territory (Where Slavery Was Prohibited) Was Not Thereby Entitled to His Freedom." Encyclopædia Britannica. Encyclopædia Britannica, inc. Accessed June 28, 2022. https://www.britannica.com/event/Dred-Scottdecision.

"US History Final Exam Study Guide (Civil War) - Quizlet Civil War Major Robert Anderson and His 86 Union Soldiers after 34 Hours."

Quizlet Inc. Accessed June 9, 2022. https://quizlet.com/176632208/us-history-finalexam-study-guide-civil-war-flash-cards/.

"Very Seldom Bought Slaves, Even Though He Owned More than 600 Slaves throughout His Lifetime." Monticello. THOMAS JEFFERSON FOUNDATION. Accessed May 29, 2022. https://www.monticello.org/slavery/slavery-faqs/property/.

"Vicksburg." American Battlefield Trust. American Battlefield Trust. Accessed August 15, 2022. https://www.battlefields.org/learn/civil-war/battles/vicksburg.

"Victory over Japan Day: End of WWII." U.S. Department of Defense. U.S. Department of Defense. Accessed June 5, 2022. https://www.defense.gov/Multimedia/Experience/VJ-Day/.

Vidar. "Jack Ruby - the Man Who Killed Lee Harvey Oswald." Medium. History of Yesterday, September 2, 2021. https://historyofyesterday.com/jack-ruby-the-man-who-killed-lee-harveyoswald-2b36b89da38d.

Wallace, Carey. "Aaron Burr in 1785, as a New York Assemblyman He, Motioned an Amendment That Called for Immediate Emancipation of All Individuals Living in Slavery." Time. Time, April 14, 2016. https://time.com/4292836/forget-hamilton-burr-is-the-real-hero/.

"Warren G. Harding Was Elected President on November 2, 1920, on His 55th." TV Tropes. thestaff@tvtropes.org. Accessed June 19, 2022. https://tvtropes.org/pmwiki/pmwiki.php/UsefulNotes/WarrenGHarding.

Warren, Perry. "John F. Kennedy Remembered: May 29, 1917 - November 22, 1963." National Portrait Gallery, January 10, 2020. https://npg.si.edu/blog/john-f-kennedy-remembered-may-29-1917%E2%80%94-november-22-1963.

Warren, Steve. "Before Memorial Day: For 50+ Years, 'Decoration Day' Was Observed to Honor and Remember Civil War Dead." CBN News. CBN News, May 30, 2022. https://www1.cbn.com/cbnnews/2020/may/before-memorial-day-for-50-years-decoration-day-was-observed-to-honorcivil-war-dead.

Weeby. "Timeline William Wilberforce." Who Am I...? Accessed June 3, 2022. https://aboutwilliamwilberforce.weebly.com/my-timeline.html.

Welle(www.dw.com), Deutsche. "May 13, 1888, Brazil Signed the Lei Aurea." DW.COM, May 13, 2018. https://www.dw.com/en/in-brazil-thewounds-of-slavery-will-not-heal/a-43754519.

"West Virginia and the Battles." National Parks Service. U.S. Department of the Interior, March 2, 2020. https://www.nps.gov/gett/learn/history-culture/civil-war-timeline.htm.

"Whig Party (United States) The Whigs Collapsed." Wikipedia, December 26, 2023. https://en.wikipedia.org/wiki/Whig_Party_(United_States).

"While Heading toward the White House, SAIC Parr Examined the President and Discovered That He Was Bleeding from the Mouth. He Directed SA Drew Unrue to Divert the Limousine to George Washington." United States Secret Service. Accessed June 30, 2022. https://www.secretservice.gov/reagan40thanniversary.

Whitaker, Morgan. "June 11, 1963: From George Wallace to John Kennedy, a Momentous Day for Civil Rights." NBCNews.com. NBCUniversal News Group, June 11, 2013. https://www.nbcnews.com/id/wbna52172836.

Whitman, Bradley H. "Andrew Jackson Passed Away." Encyclopædia Britannica. Encyclopædia Britannica, inc. Accessed May 28, 2022. https://www.britannica.com/biography/Andrew-Jackson.

"Wilberforce Was the Key Abolitionist Figure in Parliament." BBC News. BBC. Accessed June 3, 2022. https://www.bbc.co.uk/bitesize/guides/z3rj7ty/revision/8.

"William Henry Harrison." Wikipedia. Wikimedia Foundation, June 10, 2022. https://en.wikipedia.org/wiki/William_Henry_Harrison.

"William Lloyd Garrison Was an American Journalistic Crusader Who Helped Lead the Successful Abolitionist Campaign against Slavery in the United States." Biography.com. A&E Networks Television, April 22, 2021. https://www.biography.com/writer/william-lloyd-garrison.

"William McKinley Enlisted in the Union Army June 11, 1861." Encyclopedia.com. Encyclopedia.com, May 30, 2022. https://www.encyclopedia.com/history/educational-magazines/williammckinley.

"William McKinley, Sr.." geni_family_tree. Geni.com, April 29, 2022. https://www.geni.com/people/William-McKinleySr/6000000008127250348.

Williams, Yohuru. "Why Thomas Jefferson's Anti-Slavery Passage Was Removed from the Declaration of Independence." History.com. A&E Television Networks, June 29, 2020. https://www.history.com/news/declaration-of-independence-deleted-antislavery-clause-jefferson.

"Woodrow Wilson and Race in America." PBS. Accessed February 29, 2024. https://www.pbs.org/wgbh/americanexperience/features/wilson-and-race-relations/.

"Woodrow Wilsons First Wife Ellen Louise Wilson Was Born May 15, 1860, and Died, August 6, 1914." Wikipedia. Wikimedia Foundation, July 28, 2022. https://en.wikipedia.org/wiki/Ellen_Axson_Wilson.

"XIV. A General Association of Nations Must Be Formed under Specific Covenants to afford Mutual Guarantees of Political Independence and Territorial Integrity to Great and Small States Alike." National Archives and Records Administration. National Archives and Records Administration, February 8, 2022. https://www.archives.gov/milestone-documents/president-woodrow-wilsons-14-points.

Zinn Education Project. "March 30, 1870: Fifteenth Amendment." Zinn Education Project. Zinn Education Project, March 31, 2021. https://www.zinnedproject.org/news/tdih/fifteenth-amendment/.

"Political Party Timeline: 1836-1864." PBS. Accessed July 3, 2023. https://www.pbs.org/wgbh/americanexperience/features/lincolns-timeline/.